# TENTS AND TRAILS

## WILD CAMPING CHRONICLES

RATHEESH MENON

BlueRose ONE.com
Stories Matter
New Delhi • London

**BLUEROSE PUBLISHERS**
India | U.K.



BlueRose ONE.com
Stories Matter
NewDelhi • London

For permissions requests or inquiries regarding this publication, please contact:

BLUEROSE PUBLISHERS
www.BlueRoseONE.com
info@bluerosepublishers.com
+91 8882 898 898
+4407342408967

ISBN: 978-93-6783-542-5

Cover design: Yash Singhal
Typesetting: Namrata Saini

First Edition: August 2025

For

***Mittu and Reshmi***

'The two stars in my life'

# Foreword

When Ratheesh first told me he had written a book about his camping trips across India, I was immediately intrigued. And while I've known him for years, I got a true sense of his adventurous spirit on a trip to Melkotte, where we trekked to an exotic temple atop a hill in Karnataka. I still remember his enthusiasm as he explained the legends of the place, bringing history to life with every word. That same passion and sense of wonder are what you'll find on every page of this book.

As a writer, I believe the best stories aren't just about where you go, but how you see the world. In his debut travel journal, Ratheesh has a unique gift for turning a simple journey into a profound exploration. He doesn't just chronicle his adventures; he invites you into them, sharing a powerful perspective that will stay with you long after you've finished the last page.

There is a line in his book that perfectly captures the heart of his philosophy: **'I want to say one thing: if you are a human, start counting the sunrises and sunsets no matter where you live on earth and do not miss it if possible.'**

This single line is proof of the honesty and deep appreciation you'll find in these pages. It's a book that reminds us to slow down, to look closer, and to find the extraordinary in the everyday. For anyone who has ever felt the pull of the open road or simply wants to see the world from a different perspective, this book is an absolute gift. I wish him all the very best with this first book and can't wait for you, dear reader, to experience this journey for yourself.

**K. Hari Kumar**

**12 August, 2025**

# PREFACE

To portray writing a book as a humungous task, would be an understatement. Printed words get recorded into history and remain in existence until the end of the world; and as I love History, I want to be a part of it!

At the beginning I was thinking hard about what I wanted to convey through my book - what kind of experience did I want the reader to go through? That question was a hard nut to crack especially since it was my real-life camping stories and episodes laden with wildlife encounters that I wanted my readers to experience. So, I thought of keeping the major core of the book as is experience of my life and then combining a little fiction in the details to render it readable, obviously taking a slight writer's liberty as needed.

What you are going to read is the indelible impression of India's forests, wildlife and nature on the canvas of Camping with a lot of real-life incidents penned to delight the wildlife enthusiast in every one of you! This is also a sneak peek into my life – an ordinary person born in a middle-class family in the 80s who travelled across the map of India for some extraordinary experiences. Few of them I have put down here, and other remaining stories will come along with my next book delving into mysticism, supernatural and energy realms; so, wait for that.

I was blessed to travel the length of India harmoniously along with the torrential flow of nature's exploratory consciousness, as a result I was gratified to face mysterious wildlife experiences fearlessly and with an explorer's enthusiasm along the path that have been graced by great explorers and travelers since millennia. This book throws light on the 20 wonderful years of my tenting/camping experiences majorly in the mountains and forests giving me rare experiences unavailable to many in the cities. Of course, I would not want to spill anything further about the book, because that is for you readers to discover as you journey through the pages of this book.

If there is one thing I would like to underline and emphasize, it is that these natural world experiences were not anything that I went looking for. On the contrary, they sought me out through Nature's direction. That is truly what makes those experiences all the more precious. I would say it was nature's teachings for me, to understand it in depth along with its spiritual nuances.

If this book gives you an understanding that there are beautiful things beyond our mundane city or town lives right there on this earth, and that you can capture it with your five senses and also engage your sixth sense, if you are left inspired to explore the wild side of nature with mysterious experiences, if there is an awareness that comes along about the intricacies and details of mother nature, if you explore the nature around you, the game sanctuaries with more wonder and respect; I would consider this humble effort of mine a grand success.

As I grew reading a lot of wildlife accounts of Ruskin Bond, Jim Corbett, Kenneth Anderson, Ullas Karanth and the likes, you will see a lot of observations and knowledge inspired by them rendering this book also a small kind of field book of wildlife knowledge. I thank all these wildlife conservationists and also WWF India, Greenpeace, Isha Conservation, Indian Forest offices etc who have given the awareness of conservation and preservation to me and I would like to relay it across to every one of you in the best interest of our beloved Earth and the earthlings who depend on it for survival and protection. Let us also fight the greedy multi nationals, industries, bureaucrats, politicians and individuals who want to destroy nature and forests for their materialistic petty gains.

Let us not leave the fight to the green warriors rather may we all become individual green warriors fighting for our nature, because our lives, sustenance and emancipation are deeply dependent on mother nature! I offer gratitude and bows to our forests, mountains, farmers and caretakers of the natural resources because of whom I have had all these wonderful experiences which are more valuable than a billion rupees. So, let's pledge to nurture, care and grow more forests in this beautiful land India.

My sincere thanks to my family, friends and finally publishers Blue Rose for enabling me to come out with this dream of mine.

I also would like to thank each and every one of you for taking time out and reading this book. It is my wish and prayer that every moment spent with this book leaves you mesmerized with nature and you feel positively vibrant.

I hereby present this book to the world, prostrating in reverence, before the almighty Krsna for making me finally an author, a dream cherished for a long time. Please read, assimilate, reflect, enjoy and spread the word so this work can lead to many more wonderful works from my side. Thank you!

# Contents

# THE WOLF'S SNIFF!

A very warm and loving welcome to the first camping story of this book on everything and beyond tenting, wildlife encounters, and nature. I have been a crazy camping fan for close to two decades, having camped across India from Karnataka to the Himalayas in many states, mainly in wild and mountainous regions. The idea was always to get the most of Nature firsthand and celebrate nature and wildlife. This has given me so many stories and experiences that I am grateful for this adventurous spirit in a human life.

Now, without much ado, let me take you on one such camping trip I organized on New Year's Eve a few years ago in Chikamagaluru, known as the Coffee Capital of India, 272 km northwest of Bengaluru.

Chikamagaluru is a district which has existed since ancient times, proof of which are the many UNESCO heritage sites/temples in the district belonging to the Hoysala, Chalukya, and other dynasties before them. The world-famous Belur-Halebeedu temple complex, Amrutheswara temple, Kodandarama temple, and famed historical Sakrayapatna are all quite close by.

It's also famous for reserve forests like Lakkavalli, Muthodi Tiger Reserve and others. Being the biggest exporter of coffee from the country, it also has beautiful hill stations and the tallest peak in Karnataka, called Mulliangiri, standing tall at 6300 ft.

So, when I studied Engineering here a decade ago before I did this camping, we had not explored this place like we did this time as bachelors working in IT companies in Bengaluru.

The idea of this trip popped up in my mind when, after completing my treatment for my back and recuperating from my depression through Yoga in October-November of that year, I decided to dedicate the next month exclusively to travelling around Karnataka as a payback to myself for making it out of soul-sucking depression. That's a story for another day of triumph over depression and finding Yoga as a lifelong friend.

So, after visiting the erstwhile and legendary heritage places Badami-Pattadakal-Aihole in December, I decided to end the year on the $31^{st}$ with a midnight hike up forest country in Chikamagaluru by camping atop a 3500 ft tall peak in the outskirts of Chikamagaluru.

The idea for this was discussed with one of my best friends, Kodandaram, who was back from the UK after an onshore assignment. He jumped at the suggestion, as Chikamagaluru was where he grew up and studied all his life! I tagged along my younger brother Ramesh, his friend Som, and my good friend Sreejith into the adventure. The guys were excited as none had visited Chikamagaluru apart from me and Kods.

***Some information on Chikmagaluru:*** *Within a radius of 100 km, Chikamagaluru offers culture in the form of temple architecture, history, and myth, as well as coffee plantations and insights into coffee processing.*

*The journey to Chikamagaluru is always an exhilarating experience as one cruises past verdant coffee, pepper, cardamom, ginger, and coffee plantations that dot its scenic landscape. Rows of coffee bushes covered with sparkling white blossoms greet tourists, and the whole area is usually heavenly with their exquisite fragrance.*

*Chikamagaluru means 'the place of the younger daughter'. The district takes its name from the headquarters town of Chikamagaluru, which is said to have been given as a dowry to the younger daughter of Rukmangada, the legendary chief of Sakrepatna. Situated in a fertile valley south of the Baba Budan range, Chikamagaluru became the focus of global media attention when then Prime Minister Indira Gandhi, on her historic 1977 election campaign entreated the voters of the little township, "Please treat me as you would your own little daughter; I am your Chikamagalu". They gave her a thumping victory, and Chikamagaluru has since attracted the attention of adventurous travelers and nature enthusiasts. This place is an absolute treasure trove for explorers and people who like cold and chill climate!*

So, we left Bengaluru in my car after logging off early on a cold Monday evening, which was the 31st of Dec. I rented a tent, accessories and packed all other equipment I had in my camping collectibles, including my favorite hunting knife, and started the sojourn.

Now, we had left only at 5 pm and had to reach Chikamagaluru before it turned into midnight, also purchasing all the paraphernalia in terms of food, drinks, etc. We reached Hassan at 10 pm, packed all the food and beer, and zoomed off to Chikamagaluru in pitch-dark surroundings interspersed with sounds of crackers and sights of rockets from pocket villages and rural areas celebrating New Year's Eve.

We reached a lake in Chikamagaluru at 11:30 pm and saw some people celebrating with loud music on the other side of a beautiful lake. For your information, Hassan and Chikamagaluru are blessed with several lakes that are very beautiful and would be like a jewel in a drone shot (drones were unheard of during the time I am speaking).

We proceeded quickly to the mountain we were to camp on, but as it's common that you forget something key during such outings, we forgot the matchbox for setting the campfire. So, lo we rushed back to the nearest settlement, collected the matchbox and came back, and reached the foothill at half past 12 am crossing into the New Year! That drive was exhilarating to say the least.

The hill was private property, as there were coffee and oranges grown there. We parked the car somewhere in the bushes and started a hard trek up the hill amidst the vivid cacophony of crickets and owls. I could hear a barn owl go on with his calls unabatedly, which gave a mystical eerie feel to the whole environment. Now let me give you a small trivia of owls before I proceed as its one of the least understood and seen bird –

*Barn Owl found commonly*

*Referred to as the "monkey-faced owl" by some people, due to its facial features, a Barn Owl is medium-sized, with a heart-shaped face and no ear-tufts. Distributed worldwide, these pale-colored owls have been named Barn Owls owing to their traditional use of barn lofts and church steeples as nesting sites.*

*Barn owls are very elusive nocturnal hunters, although it is not uncommon to see them emerge at dusk or active at dawn, and very occasionally in-flight during daylight.*

**Calls and Hunting:** *Even though Barn owls have excellent vision at dawn, they depend on their skill of hearing to hunt. Unlike other owls, Barn owls do not hoot, but they vocalize by screeching very loudly and using raspy calls. The courtship call is a shrill, repetitive twittering.*

There was a hoot of another owl, something like hollow-sounding notes with the last calls in rapid succession. This was really something interesting, giving me a feel of clairaudience in the tranquil silence of the estate forest! The silence descended on us; a bit eerie yet interestingly mystical. An occasional call of the peacock was a reassuring one, but that was in long gaps and few. We had to pitch our tents sooner, so we could sit down in peace and fill the empty stomachs and parched throats.

The hike was very steep, so we could hear each other's panting and puffing as we scaled forward. We took a few breaks and made use of the breaks to pluck Oranges and stuff our bags! And listen to all the nocturnal calls of a wide variety of small fauna, especially birds and insects. And now, as luck would have it, at a gnarled old tree enroute that had a hollow at the juncture where its trunk branched out into a lopsided Y, I saw a little owl at 5 ft height, and it was peeking out, looking at us with its big round *ullu* eyes! The nocturnal bird looked hauntingly beautiful and brilliant. I had a good glimpse, as did the others from a distance, and continued our walk.

The sky was turning up well with the full moon in glow, a lot of stars for company and a mild breeze flowing from the west to northeast. The leaves on the trees were rustling with the flow of the wind. I could make it out because I was keeping track of my compass and checking the wind flow as well. It was a breezy night with great natural lighting and the perfect cold weather to add on to the ambiance. My thermal t-shirt underneath was helping, I guess the temperature was around 14 to 15 degrees. The thermal pants, though, were giving out heat as I was sweating from the trek effort.

In the near distance I could hear the howling of a dog as I thought! The ground was strewn with boulders and pebbles, making the climb a bit challenging in the night. The crickets and cicadas were singing their loud chorus, as we passed through dense foliage one after the other. I picked up a stick to act as a trek stick, which also could be used to create some commotion during the walk to drive off small snakes which are nocturnal too; you never know if one is lying somewhere enroute, so it's better to be aware than aloof.

As I had climbed a major portion of the hill, it struck me that firewood would be necessary for the campfire, and it may not be available at the top. So, I pulled out my classical hunting knife gifted by my dear friend Swapnil in 2006; after he was thankful for the brilliant trek, we went on the Sakleshpur-Subramanya forest rail route (which is an adventure story for another day). But I definitely need to mention that, it is one of the best treks in Karnataka!

The knife was damn good and useful in cutting branches and stems, making up the firewood. I used it like a ninja to cut and distribute the firewood to all other guys, and we carried it through. Finally, after another 20-minute climb, we were at the camping spot, which was a flat area albeit not the peak which was in mind. The peak was still a 10-minute climb ahead and was fully rocky. At least here we had the mud and grass needed for pitching the tent, using the pegs.

Out came the tent for the night and the beers. With an occasional sip, we started pitching the conventional tent which was new to a couple of the boys among us. We were 5 in number, so two were asked to set the dinner from the parcels and arrange it.

I, Kods, and Sreejith started joining the sticks together and getting the pegs nailed on the ground. There was a fair breeze blowing, blowing away the tent a bit; so Sreejith had to hold the crossbow sticks atop for us to tie the ropes to the pegs.

With the cold breeze, it brought an idea of a hot tea before dinner! So, out came the burner stove and matchbox. As the water was brimming, the conversations caught fire and spread into various topics in the cold ambiance. The dinner was bought as piping hot biryani, chicken fry and mushroom dry; but by the time it was opened after 3 hours, it was cold but inviting while being served.

Tea was the only hot beverage we had now, so it flowed down our throats like *amrit* down a yearning throat accompanied by the conversations. Let me tell you this secret of an adventurous life; that fresh and novel conversations are like nectar to the adventure outing you have. They are like the juicy ripe pineapple essence in our city-based lives of monotony and boredom; more so if the company and people are new!

All through this, we also got the campfire going using the firewood and brake oil that were brought atop. The campfire was essential considering the cold and ambiance it renders and to drive away wild animals if any!

It was time for dinner and drinks; all the soft drinks and fried chicken along with some snacks came out. The food festival began with the relaxed, sumptuous dinner.

The campfire was burning bright, throwing out gleams of pleasant yellow light streaks and warmth. All through this there was heavy disturbance of yelling and abuses from up above the mountain. There were some boys who had camped atop the peak, which was a 15-minute walk uphill. They were drunk and spoiling the mood of the beautiful, breezy night. But we ignored them as if they were barking mongrels.

Sitting in front of the tent in a semi-circle facing the campfire, we were very joyful, forgetting the entire year that had been and diving into the moment with laughter and giggles. On the other side of the hill where we were, there was a series of majestic tall hills watching silently as the New Year's Eve slipped by.

Discussions and stories were yarned first about personal lives by all; and then about local legends, places by Kods, as he was from this town and had spent his school and college life here. It was quite enchanting to know more about Chikamagaluru and its mountains, coffee estates, and the stories of people there.

Meanwhile, I too had a few stories up my sleeves, as I too had studied here, and Kods and I were college mates from AIT, Chikamagaluru. We had quite some interesting stuff to reminisce about from the vast data bank of college stories involving friends and lecturers/ professors. Most were travel stories on bikes we could lay hands on and zoom off after bunking classes.

There were funny stories with wit and cultural-generational coloring. As the talks continued, I felt the need to look up at the skies. And boy was it an astonishing sight to behold – the Moon was full and brimming with splendor, there was a small halo around the moon, and then a bigger, wider halo formed the outer concentric circle! It was very defined and mystical, and one could look at it for hours on end! This part of nature is what makes camping in the wilderness special and sidereal as it was on this day.

I called the boys and pointed out the beauty to the amazement of everyone, just when I heard a faint howl. The ESP (extra sensory perception) in me was telling me to have a look around to ascertain if it was a dog, as dogs were unlikely here owing to the houses being far away, and a stray dog in the absence of food will not come up so high. Curiosity got the better of me and I just drifted into the woods with my torch as others were watching the sky. As I had been there cutting and collecting firewood some time ago, I was confident. Pointing my torch in high beam across to the farthest area, I scanned slowly for any hints of a wild animal; and lo I could see two faint reflections albeit looking like dots. This vanished as I panned and then came back to the same spot with the torch beam. I suspected it to be a wild creature, probably a wild boar. I continued the torch scan for a couple of minutes more, but then I heard a few huffs and puffs, albeit coming from slightly afar. I walked further, confused with the uncertainty, and reached a rock on the ground; pointing my torch I could see that it was a big drop a step further. Carefully scanning the area and gulping down a small amount of fear I ventured further. Although it is a bit risky as it falls near the tiger sanctuary and hyenas lurk in the area, which I was unaware as I went ahead. The calls-hoots of the owl and cicadas were loud and ambient, and I was enjoying the silence of the night, cajoled in between by the soft, cold breeze. Walking further, I came across a *nalla*, or a stream, flowing on the right side of the path, but this was now quite a bit far from the campsite. I decided to turn back as I was not getting a hint of anything that I thought, just as I turned around, I heard a heavy sniff! This was followed by a sudden flight of a big bird; I turned my head to realize it was a big eagle owl with quite a big wingspan. I was instantly reminded of the big migratory owl I saw in my father's office when I was a kid in 5$^{th}$ standard; that came to the office premises and was captured, kept for 2 days for viewing and handed over to the forest department. After that day this was the second time, I was seeing such a huge owl! Reminiscing of this I continued a few more steps when I heard the deep resonant booming call of the same owl nearby, but this time the fear got the better of me and I decided to turn back tracing the path I traversed. Panting heavily, in under ten minutes I reached the camp site. Sreejith curiously enquired where I had wandered off; I brushed his quip and joined back to the party. They all were downing a second beer recounting the memorable moments of everyone's year gone by.

I was a bit aloof thinking on the eyes I saw, when Som snapped and started a melody fit for the moment. The popular number from the past – *"Ye shaam mastani madhahosh kiye jaaye, mujhe dor koi kheeche teri aur liye jaaye!"* This was a jolly good number and a nice rendition of the melody making all of us sway in fun.

Slowly the night deepened, the campfire weakened, and the boys' sleep thickened. The Moon was sitting snugly in the sky and the mountains behind and around us stood silent and magnificent. The jungle was still whispering like a silent pandemonium. Excitement to see the sunrise next morning was very high for me, as I had seen the sight of sunrise the last time I camped here, with a bigger group way back in 2009.

Meanwhile, pleasantries went up to past 2 O'clock when the cold became deeper, and the boys went inside the tent seeking the sleeping bags; they dozed off for a while. The campfire crackled softly beneath the star-filled sky. I rekindled the fire and put in more firewood for a few more hours of fire. Kods and I had our bodies inside the tent and the heads outside staring at the stars and moon counting the constellations, planets ever aware that shooting stars are common sight over this part of the country.

Cicadas and crickets were still a chorus although to a lesser extent at this time of the night, and few fireflies hovered in the area nearby before they vanished into the thick night.

Now it was our zone of college discussions and adventures of yesteryears of the biking we did, the mountains we hiked and traversed! Swapping stories the night grew darker and chillier, giving a feeling of such pristine joy like nothing else. The bliss of camping is one of a kind which cannot be expressed in words or phrases, it must be felt and experienced to be relished. This close to nature is a portion of eternity and contentment. The amore of nature unbound by the mind can be touched with camping in the wild and diving into the ecstasy of Mother Nature!

It's a no-mind zone which is a gift for adventure travelers to explore and feel the world around them. For instance, knowing that two Tiger sanctuaries Lakkavalli and Muthodi are not far gives that mysterious touch to the night, reminding that a leopard or tiger could be anywhere in proximity and probably keeping a watch on us.

Conversing in between and passing the rest of the time in blunt wonder of the celestial sights, time passed, and it was 4.20 am in the morning. We didn't feel an iota of sleep when I looked at the watch but suggested a quick nap to Kods. We drifted to sleep quite quickly, and then when it felt I was in between a long blissful nap - I heard shooing and unabated shouting by my friend!!

I woke up with a startle and sat up to behold the sight of a dark grey-white colored Wolf combined with black shades sniffing at the left over and strewn Biriyani lying 6 ft away! The wolf was well lit by the campfire and its gray fur shimmering under the moonlight, showing it in considerable detail!

I froze; my heart started pounding and it took me a while to realize it was a wolf.

Now a sight of a wolf in India where it's mostly extinct, and the wild stories heard over years render a great importance to the sighting when it is least expected! And so, we were thrilled as much as afraid at the sight of the visitor which is an endangered species in India. As with common city folks who have only seen the wolf in movies or zoos, we were considerably scared because of the ignorance of the behavioral patterns of a wolf.

It was a moment when the wolf stared at us with those two deep and investigative eyes with the head shifted to the right side; the two black marks under the eyes enhanced the stare to an eerie level.

The black pupils were drilling in as if anticipating something. The brief moment brought all the Mowgli and jungle stories and visuals watched on TV to mind! It was totally unlike a dog with a touch of mystic element.

So, we got defensive and tried shooing/shouting it away, to which it was confused in the beginning but a little later responded with a display of its teeth in defense - *grrr…!!!* We knew that a lone wolf is always a coward, so Kodu grabbed a stone nearby and threw at it with a force as if it were a werewolf! It evaded the throw and ran away, irritated by the shooing and shouting or probably confused about what to do.

*Indian grey wolf*

As it ran, I recollected my good senses and reminded Kods that it was a wonderful moment for a photograph, and we have 2 DSLRs one being a full frame Canon. We jumped to our feet and brisked with the torch in hand. Rushing the foliage for a click for posterity's sake, but we could not sense which way it might have vanished. We followed the path a few yards down the lane, then we heard a commotion in the right direction. A stone hit by my feet rumbled down creating some considerable noise – and I noticed couple of pairs of glowing eyes in the distance, two were low to the ground and the other two were 1 foot high. They were unblinking and watching us intently. We affirmed that it was the wolf.

Now, it was clear that the wolf had come to fetch food for its younger one. It stood still for a couple of minutes, and then just turned and ran with the small one into the dark.

Meanwhile, kods managed to click a pic in hurry but to the dismay, as the mode was manual and he did not get time to adjust the light setting, it came as few light dots on a dark patch. Nevertheless, we managed to see an animal which was rare, seldom seen in the wild at close range and recognized it as the Indian grey wolf; that was a dopamine moment!

We returned to the tent in the chilly climate outside accompanied by the whisper of the breeze. The other boys were sleeping crisscross blissfully, aloof to whatever happened outside. We both sat discussing for some time about the wolf and other animals like Hyenas that could be lingering in the area, and Muthodi had quite a few of them. Recounting other stories Kods had known of wildlife since his childhood we drifted into early dawn. One such story was about a Hyena who was a constant dog lifter from an area bit down the south of where we were camping. That Hyena had become a menace in estate houses preying on dogs and goats; after a considerable number of complaints to the DFO of Muthodi forest, the wildlife authorities came and tracked it down and relocated it to Lakavalli forest on the way to Shimoga.

Further far away in Muthodi forests and Kemmangundi ranges, it was tiger country - which campers are a bit weary of. In that sense I can say that

Chikamagaluru is a beautiful tourist place with History, Heritage temples, Estates (Coffee), Forests, Wildlife, Waterfalls, Mountains and chilly climate to top it all. So, it is an ideal place which never loses its charm.

Another quite common animal was the leopard, as he could lay easy hands on the livestock of small villages and hamlets from Chikamagaluru area to the Kadur ranges. All these predators mainly preyed on wild hens, hares, goats, dogs and peacocks which roamed freely in the estates.

We thought of making some tea as our sleep was a lost cause now. The climate was extremely cold now and my teeth were chattering relentlessly while making the tea. The Assam tea bags gave us strong tea needed to kick start early in the morning. We waited for an hour for the clock to click 6 a.m. and then wake the others up. They wanted to see the sunrise as much as we did. So, we made tea and warmed them to the wolf story that happened a few hours ago. They were startled and astonished as they had only heard attacking stories of wolves from books and movies.

Sreejith was curious about its looks and features, whereas Som was concerned if it's dangerous and will be still around as a pack or group. The way we answered them of its appearance and how wonderful it was to see an endangered species who used to be in abundance in the past in India. Their dread was replaced with curiosity and interest. So, this being all of our first experience of wildlife encounter leaving the elephant experiences most south Indians have had; we were basking in the adventure that happened.

Meanwhile Kods and I along with Sreejith started wrapping up the tents as we did not want the rented tents to be left unattended and go up. We packed up and started the climb to the peak, which was a 15 min steep climb, but boy oh boy the increase in cold and the early rays of the Sun gave that big jolt of energy surge which was exhilarating to say the least.

As we reached the top the hooligan boys who were shouting all night long seemed to have become sober and just side walked us and went down. Now, the peak was for us, and the sight was one to behold – Mountains forming a crested jewel all around, the valley to the east dense with thick foliage was getting washed with the bright light orange rays of the Sun.

The rock face atop had some remains of the overnight campfire the locals had put up. I sat around it to get some warmth as it was as cold as in the Himalayas - probably 5 degrees. I recalled the memories of my Tapovan camping in Gangotri National Park a few years ago.

The Sunrise which manifested that day morning as I was warming by is the best Sunrise in my life for sure, considering the purest orange shade and light I have ever seen and bathed by, the vistas in front to behold in terms of the endless forest, line of mountains, Coffee and Orange estates, and pristine villages interspersed here and there.

*View of forests from the side of mountain we camped*

The rock on which we were, was high on energy as I could sense the energy it was radiating with the first rays of the sun (as though it was waiting all night to welcome the new year Sun with pomp and fervor). Why I say I could sense the energy is because all through my life I have been drawn to rocks and there is a silent extra sensory energy exchange I have had with rocks and mountains.

Rocks represent the raw energy of the core of the earth and mountains attract so much universal pranic energy that their vibration is very high. Moreover, our culture has always believed that even rocks and mountains have life in them albeit being inanimate to our eyes.

Our Indian sculpture science or Shilpa kala goes ahead to say that rocks have male, female and transgender sexes just like humans. And all great architect-sculptors like Jakanachari from ancient Karnataka and Perumthachan from ancient Kerala used to test the rocks and select them for the sculpture. As a matter of fact, they could also determine the music in the stone or sculpt it to make musical rock pillars as seen in Hampi.

The images that I saw are one of a kind depicting the raw beauty of Western ghats and Chikamagaluru as a mountainous beauty. We gathered around the campfire remains and started warming our hands to the soft warmth of the smoke and amber wood, on the verge of burning out.

I pulled out my hunting knife and posed for a few nice images for posterity, which was soon taken over by Ramesh and Sreejith for acrobatic poses with the knife. The photo vanity soon took over with some pleasantries thrown on the jumps and fitness of each poser, till we had enough and decided to climb down to the parking space at the foothills.

As we were descending, we heard the pristine and melodious calls of so many morning birds along with peacock calls, that I could say this alone makes me come back to the mountains and nature as a retreat for myself. The descent was easy and fast. We plucked a few ripe oranges to gorge on during the climb down, treating the selves to citrus blast in the morning.

At the foothill the car was covered in dew and mist and a lot of fallen leaves. I cleaned it tediously and started loading the camp equipment and luggage to the boot. I powered up the engine, heard a few revs and was quite ready to head out before the estate workers came.

The soft vroom of the engine gave a pleasant feeling to drive back through the scenic misty mountains and beautiful roads to the town, reminiscing of the adventurous night with the wolf! Looking forward to the next camping adventure we headed back to Bangalore.

**Wolf Trivia:**

*Wolves generally work hard to avoid humans. But still a wolf's most powerful weapon is his mouth, equipped with large teeth and strong jaws. Its bite is quite powerful and once it tastes human flesh, it is found to become a man-eater, hunting small children in packs. It can even crush the bones and digest just like Hyenas.*

*The Indian wolf is a species moving towards extinction and the government or sanctuaries are not much bothered about their rehabilitation and protection. Karnataka is one place where they are found, specifically in Chikamagaluru district, Koppal district, jowar fields in north Karnataka like Gulbarga, Melukote Wildlife Sanctuary in Mandya District, Ranebennur and Daroji Wildlife Sanctuaries etc. They are also found in Black buck sanctuaries like Maidenahalli near Madhugiri of Tumkur district, as they prey on Blackbucks.*

*Predominantly, wolves in Karnataka and elsewhere are found in Territorial Forest Divisions, which do not have management plans for wildlife. Worse still, a lot of wolf habitat is revenue land, which can be apportioned overnight for all manner of development activities with no concern for its fauna or flora. Wolves are "disappearing predators" in two ironic ways. First, they can melt in the brown and grey hues of arid regions and quickly move out of sight. This allows them to share space with people but from a safe distance. Second, despite this strategy, their survival in human-use areas has become increasingly difficult. They are threatened by domestic dogs and occasional persecution by people. But most importantly, the arid habitats they occupy are undergoing rapid unsustainable change in the form of water-intensive agriculture, energy infrastructure, and tree plantations. This diminishing space affects biodiversity and wolf populations will, unfortunately, disappear if this continues unabated.*

# THE CURIOUS BEAR OF TUMKUR!

Tumkur the mountain land, I welcome you there which is as ancient as Karnataka and as young as an adventurer's spirit! This is a land of many temples, history, caves, wildlife reserves, forests, important mountain peaks and a lot of mysticism as well.

Let me take you to one such hill called Siddharabetta - which translates to hill of the Siddhas (mystics). The hilltop is famous for a beautiful series of caves which has a perennial source of water and a Shiva Linga inside. Sages and mystics have been living here in the cave ever since the earliest records of Tumkur. Even today one can find siddhas and monks from north called Naga Babas who have made the Tumkur hilltops and caves their meditation homes.

The story of the camping I'm going to narrate is one that occurred in 2018 with my colleagues from Tata Power. I and Ravishankar, the adventurous bear among us, wanted to go camping in the wild country. So, one evening as we were having tea in the breakout area, I suggested Siddharabetta as it can offer cave exploration followed by camping atop the hill. We pitched the idea to boys in the team who were novice in this respect, and it was an affirmative yes from all.

So, on the Friday before the camping, we went to Bommasandra and picked all the adventure gear including camping burners and tents from an adventure gear renting company. The spirits of myself and Ravi were very high as this was camping after a long time. I for one was elated beyond normal as since marriage I had not done camping in the wild in Karnataka. The few camping instances I had were in Uttarakhand in Gangotri National Park, and it was safe as wildlife is less over there.

So, we gathered next morning in my car and 1 bike and zoomed off to Tumkur. This was a pleasant drive through erstwhile countryside with farms all along. We reached Dabaspete picked up few brake oils for camping from there and had the famous Davanagere benne dose (butter dosa) for breakfast. After licking the fingers clean and washing down the throat with a piping hot tea, we resumed the remaining drive with a boost in the enthusiasm.

Driving and riding through the offbeat rural areas of Tumkur filled with farms and pastures, we reached the foothills of Siddharabetta by afternoon. The climb that was staring at us was a moderately steep one and the problem was a couple of guys were non-climbers. They had to huff and puff through to attempt the climb and get going. A note to all those who consider themselves young, please attempt a good steep climb in Karnataka or Maharashtra and then evaluate your youth for yourself. In India they say from ages that one is as young as their spine and legs!

Now, coming back to the outing; everyone started the climb with a wonder as the prospect of a big series of connected caves was quite inviting. The ones who were decently fit climbed it easily amidst the thick foliage of the trees - all through the climb. The other two who were alien to climbing were struggling as said before.

We could see a lot of versatile birds enroute, climbing with the company of their calls was quite soothing and attuning to nature; one specifically to be mentioned is the Rufous treepie with its calls and dance! As we reached the top, the flat top was beaming with monkeys of all sizes (common macaques). They were jumping and playing around as if they were school children out on a picnic. There was a Sadhu (saint) sitting right outside the mouth of the cave with a paraphernalia of spiritual items for sale. He was a dark-complexioned aged man around 65-70 years with very sharp eyes having a greyish circle around the pupil. His moustache and beard were very natural, grey-black and flowing adding on to his persona.

He looked at us with a pleasant grin. Pointing to us the cards he had spread out in front of him; he asked me to sit down for a tete-a-tete. I obliged with pleasure as he had info on Hinduism (Sanatana Dharma) spread out on the cloth. I am a great fan of the eternal Hindu Culture and Spirituality, so all the merrier! But I first enquired with him about the cave and if we can enter it and explore it, to which he replied, "*magu*, (son, in Kannada) the cave is closed for exploration last year due to an untoward incident which happened inside; so now there is only the access to the *Shiva linga* at the entrance." I asked what the incident was, to which he responded that some young guy took a girl inside and molested her after which the police caught the culprit and subsequently closed the cave to the public.

I brought the boys mainly for the cave exploration which is a long series of caves with a lot of cave rooms dedicated to Sadhus/munis who come during the year and make it their dwelling spot for meditation and sadhana. So, I had wanted to meet some sadhu this time around which was not possible now. Now, such uncultured youth or culprits always spoil the sanctity or accessibility of such places by their criminal activities, which is a very unfortunate thing in the culture capital of the world - India. But who can give sense to such anti-social elements in a vast country bustling with raw population! Resigning ourselves to disappointment, we thought the trip was in vain, so the guys grouped under a small roof and were discussing other options.

I chose to continue speaking to the Sadhu. He asked me a few questions on the sampradayas and to which I belonged, followed by Gotra and the subsequent details. I was found wanting because I knew only my gotra. Also, the philosophies which Hindus follow were detailed by him; everyone is free to choose one like Adwaita, Dwaita, Vishishtadwaita etc..So, it was a crash course for me and I was intrigued by his knowledge and his penchant for settling down there to make Hindus aware of the same.

I commended his tough decision to leave his family in old age for spirituality's sake which is not easy; come there atop a mountain, sell a few spiritual commodities and spend his life educating the society. He was not pushy for selling his stuff; he told, "if you purchase then I can buy some grains, else I will go gain it by bhiksha yajana (alms request) from the village down. I now had a soft corner and admiration for this elderly man.

The other guys were obviously not very inclined, they being of much younger blood. So, they were chit chatting under a thatched shelter and making merry. Now, as I enquired with the old man for a campsite, he told me there's no place to pitch on top and that we would have to go down and that too be silent even if we pitch the tent somewhere at the foothill. Now this was not possible as camping comes with chats, discussions and debates which inherently are noisy. So, I told we will continue to explore areas around the hill and not pitch the tent on Siddharabetta or rather check at the foothill.

Before leaving I asked the guys if I could meditate for 15 minutes, to which they obliged. Just then it started drizzling very lightly, and there were a lot of monkeys playing around near the saddhu. I decided to sit on the rocky floor beside the saddhu facing the monkeys and do my kriya meditation which was kind of an intuitive decision. Why I want to tell you this is because, acts of mediation are sometimes spontaneous and energy-ambiance driven.

Keeping my eyes partially open I drifted into the meditative space to the accompaniment of monkey circus around! The beautiful sight of the mountains and valleys ahead, along with the overcast sky with semi-dark clouds, was just a magical ambiance to meditate in. All through the meditation thoughts kept coming in and playing like the monkeys who were jumping around; I sat witness to the thought monkeys and the real ones, enjoying the paraphernalia of the play that is the mind. Slowly as the time was up, I warmed up, got up and joined the boys after a good meditation. I want to highlight that it's important to open up to the energy of any mountain or space through meditation or sitting still when you are there. This makes the experience a deeper and profound one.

Now, we had this important question as to where to pitch the tent for which the entire trip was planned, and things rented. Ravi was very curious and did not want to camp in a noise sensitive spiritual area. So, I decided to take a drive around the foothills into the villages and nearby locations to spot a campsite.

We descended quickly as the dusk was approaching, drank tea at the tea shop and zoomed off in the car to hunt the camp spot. On the way I saw the forest office which gave me a bolt of jitter as they might be patrolling, and they might not permit me to enter the camp. I thought of approaching for permission but then thought otherwise and took a right turn from the junction to head to some inland areas. The guys on the bike were following my car as I was the lead.

I was a bit tensed about finding the spot in an hour as after dark it becomes very difficult to find one.

Driving further, we scanned places for pitching the tent driving through dense green areas but none seemed suitable. Meanwhile, the guys on the bike drove ahead and we lost communication with them. Suddenly they came rushing by and were very elated to find a spot. Uday told, "bro you will definitely like it, and it's secluded from the public road; also, there is a small concrete structure covering the area where we can pitch the tent".

I was so happy and elated to learn this and immediately turned the car to head there asap. As a bit more delay would have ensured no camping on the day! We reached there in a jiffy; to my pleasant surprise it was sunset time, and the place was a gigantic rocky hill a little high above the elevation of the road, but was kind of hidden. This was like multiple campsites on a platter. I could see the sun set splendidly behind the rocky flat hill.

The campsite was perfect: a rocky outcrop perched a few feet above the ground and surrounded by mountains. It was obvious that this rock would be the only warm place in this cold area at night; and animals would love to warm themselves up on the rock. I presumed that leopards, bears and other animals would flock here in the night, which was an eerie but adventurous thought (there were boards along the road indicating the animals' presence).

Brushing the thought aside we took the car through the rocks like a 4*4 vehicle and parked it behind the small building which had a peepal tree beside it. The building was rejoicing in the shade of the peepal tree. As I stood observing the beauty of the tree for a moment, I saw the gentle rustling leaves of the peepal tree flutter and tremble in their thousands as if in torment, moved by the currents of warm evening air that cross each other or intermingle as they drift down from the lofty crags of the rocky area.

The day's golden hues had faded into a serene twilight, but we were losing time for pitching the tent. Just glancing around, I could see the orange-crimson sky enhancing the beauty of the two triangular hills and the forest all around. I thought to myself, I am in a South Indian jungle inhabited sparsely by few villages here and there and sufficiently abundant wildlife for company. Night had fallen by this time and the sky in all its hue, a scintillating mantle apparently in unceasing movement, caused by the twinkling of myriads of stars was a pleasant delight. There was no moon in sight yet, even though it was touted to be a moony night as per google sky app.

Ravi called me just then to speed up the tent pitching, in this case it was not the conventional pitching as it was a rock, and we had to put the tents and place some rocks as pegs on them. Ravi and Santosh got busy unfolding the two wildcraft tents in tandem. Slowly the light faded out before completion of setting the tent, leaving us in a spot; I ran to the car and switched on the car's high beam to assist the pitching. This made the activities easier, and we proceeded with the campfire set up after that. In the six of us conventional tent setup was new to 4 of them, who were keen to see it and get involved.

Now reality hit us as we were starting the campfire set up. The brake oil bottles needed to ignite the campfire were missing. Ravi asked me, "Anna, where is the brake oil I gave you at the shop". I had totally lost track of that and tried accessing my memory files to realize that I had kept them in the dosa shop desk where we sat for food. Now, this was a big problem as it was a bit windy, and we needed some fuel to get the fire going. Dry grass was hardly available and the paper I fetched from the car was not sustainable to build a fire.

I quipped that we have two cans of cooking fuel which we could capitalize on, to which I got a placid response from Ravi. We needed the fuel for the small stove for cooking, so there had to be a compromise and wise usage of it for both purposes. As that was the only retort, I dug out the small fuel cans from the accessory bag. With the building fire, I poured the fuel onto it slowly as this fuel was a spontaneous fire oil and not a lasting one.

It took quite some effort from all of us, especially Santosh to build and get the fire going. Santosh brought out his village childhood skills to the fore to build a good fire. We got firewood from the branches of the small thick shrubs with strong trunks nearby. This was a bit eerie and challenging as the fear of an animal was high in the darkness; so, using the mobile torches we cut a few branches laboriously to feed the campfire which was done frequently as these were bush branches and not thick tree branches. I understood for a fact that firewood selection, cutting and collection is not a meagre or easy task. This is done as a full-time profession by many in Indian villages and forests, as they run a lot of household chores and cook using the precious firewood.

As soon as we got a good fire going with embers showing up, we put a hold on the firewood gathering and concentrated on setting up the cooker. The cooking fuel was not plenty, so it had to be used judiciously and frugally to get us the cooked food. Now, we had bread, some ketchup, jams, eggs and Maggi. This looked ok to all but Uday and Sudarshan, who wanted rice and substantial food to fill their empty stomachs.

Getting rice or any food from the hotel nearby was an unlikely affair considering we were in the middle of a forest area; and the next village or inhabitation could be very far considering we could see no lights for a long distance as much as the eyes could see. But both were adamant and did not listen to my persuasion to settle with the food we had. I warned them of the dangers of going in the dark in an uncertain forest area; but to no avail as their stomachs were ruling their heads.

At last, fed up with their ranting, I had to give up, advising some warnings to keep in mind. They zoomed off in the bike taking a right turn into the forest road. I could track them for a few hundred meters through the bike's headlight, slowly losing track of the bike. I just hoped they would come back safely even without food.

An hour had passed and there was no whereabouts of the boys, so I continued helping Santosh build the fire and sustain it with a lot of twigs and branches from the dry deciduous shrubs nearby. The distant call of a nightjar provided a soothing soundtrack. The eerie silence of the night was broken by this bird and soon Ravi's jokes and his lively ghost stories filled the campsite. He had many things to tell from his stay at Hyderabad and his sojourns in Ladakh. Just as we were in the middle of an interesting Djinn story, I heard the whooshing sound of a bike; to which I ran and stood on the rock overseeing the road below. To my dismay it was a local villager on a motorbike.

A few minutes passed by in silence and then I could hear a stronger bike sound approaching, this time as I went and stood on the rock, I could breathe a sigh of relief as it were the boys. I went down behind the car, there was a large flat rock where the boys came and parked the bike.

They were excited and frightened at the same time. They were perplexed as well, as I could sense from their tone, "bro, bro you know what? What you said was correct; we should have listened to you!"

I enquired why they were so frightened, literally shivering. Uday told, "Bro, there are a lot of bears around and that too rogue ones. We went riding some distance to find no shops or villages, as we continued riding there was a small village with some lights; we went to a small shop open there to ask for food. That's when a middle-aged man sitting there warned us to return immediately to the place we came from, as there were a lot of bears and there was an attack on a man riding a bike in the night, just the previous week. He scared the shit out of us, as the man sustained major injuries. On his insistence we promised him to return once we got some food for our hungry stomachs. So, he guided us to the next village 5 km down the village road beside a series of hills to a small restaurant. We followed as told and reached the place, luckily there was some egg rice and curry left. We made the shop guy pack it along with some egg bhurji. He too was concerned that we were alone in the night and that we had to ride through the forest and mountains some 15 odd kilometers. We told him that we were going straight to our stay, and we immediately started our bike in earnest and headed back."

I was becoming more impatient and at the same time interested in the story unfolding. Now Sudharshan took over, "bro, the return journey was one of the scariest in our lives. We had to ride through the same forest region with hills this time slowly and more vigilantly, which took a long time. We were anticipating a bear at every crossroad or road bends. In between we heard a few noises, stopped the bike every time to ensure it was not a bear or leopard. We being new to this, it was even more anxiety ridden and fearful ride on the way back. The darkness was really eerie and we had to rely on the average headlights to reach here. It really was an edge of the seat horror movie kind of experience and thank God we reached here safely. But all the way through all kinds of animal stories and ghost stories were playing in our head bro!"

I was relieved now that their story did not have a serious bear encounter, phew!

We assembled in front of the tent and spread the food out. Uday and Santosh started cooking the Maggi noodles. Soon, the noodles were ready and fuming with steam. Bringing the bread, Egg and rice we started having our dinner. This was going to be a very memorable dinner considering the camping and ambiance around in a forest under the starry sky. For few of them it was first in their lives, adding an extra tinge of thrill and adventure!

The medium masala laden food was enjoyed by all sumptuously. The campfire was dying down, so we had to bring more firewood from the branchy shrubs nearby. So, three batches of two people each went fetching firewood with a torch each. The villagers' account of the bear stories was playing in the mind all along making the firewood cutting a thrilling experience. Just then Uday heard some commotion nearby which was considerable and eerie! He called me with a whisper, which made me rush to the spot leaving the warmth of the flickering flame.

Now, I sat down with my ear close to the ground to sense any vibration. Just 2 minutes and I could hear a faint rustling from the nearby bushes. We stayed put to find what that was, even though our legs wanted to run to the safety of the tent and stay locked in. But we had come for adventure and how can someone leave such an adrenaline rush unanswered?!

Life was too predictable back in the city and corporate offices, barring the ego surprise from our imbecile bosses! So, we stayed put without a wink and not making any noise barring the smooth breathing which went on unabated. The rustling was just one off and did not recur thereafter, we stood/sat there for a good ten minutes to hear nothing. Uday sighed and walked off in exasperation. I tried signaling him not to make any noise, but the signal reached deaf ears. I could see all four guys looking towards my direction from the campfire asking me what it was. As I could not figure out anything, I just waved that it was nothing but my imagination.

As I reached the campfire, I heard the faint hoot of an owl, and the crickets started chirping again. We returned to our ghost stories and this time it was Ravi narrating the story of a Djinn from a mansion in old Hyderabad. This was an interesting story which I would detail in another book of mine on horror stories. But the gist was that Ravi and friends had gone on bike to explore an old mansion in old Hyderabad in the night time. They lost their way and reached a dead end and were searching how to get out, just when they saw an old lady looking like a gypsy coming their way as if to say something; but she walked past without saying anything, so they called the lady, and she turned back. She had light brownish eyes with heavy mascara and ornate jewelry which did not go well with her loose and somewhat torn clothes. She had lush hair interspersed with grey hair strands which were neat and groomed.

Ravi's friend asked for directions to the nearest habited place, to which she smiled and grinned mystically. Ravi asked her again saying they are lost and she pointed to the right. Ravi and friends thanked her and went pondering as to who she was, found in an area where no one else was there.

They reached a cross junction, confused, they took a right to reach another right turn to the left of which was an old mansion named Navi Haveli. Ravi jumped in excitement as this was the mansion they were searching for. They saw that the gate was rusted and locked with an age-old lock. Adjacent to it there was a climbable wall, which was inviting to climb. They obliged and crossed the wall and walked towards the mansion which looked quite like the mansion from some English movies. It had tinted windows and the mansion was painted in Casablanca yellow which stood faded and worn out. Just when they were about to peep in, they heard an *"oye"* sound from behind. Turning back, they saw an old security guard calling out to them in an angry pitch. Walking towards the guard they grinned at him to get a frown as response. The guard enquired what they were doing there in the late evening. Ravi said, "Anna, we have heard about this haunted mansion and wanted to check it out to write a story in our college magazine." The guard was not convinced and with some concern told them that it was a dangerous place inhabited by Djinns and there were many stories since a century claiming sighting of the Djinns and strange happenings. He told them, no humans came to this area which was quite large and cut-off after 6 pm for a long time. He was posted there by the owner of the properties to keep a watch till night sets in. He also told them to be wary of anyone looking out of the ordinary in the vicinity; and that they should get out of there immediately and reach their respective places without stopping in between.

The boys, now quite scared and puzzled, told him about the old gypsy kind of woman they saw and how she was different and mystical at the same time. He immediately asked about her appearance. On hearing the appearance and about the attire, he was shocked. As a reflex he asked them to leave immediately and that he too is leaving. On enquiring why, he told, "*Beta, vo budau aurat Djinn hai* (that old lady is a Djinn), *hum inke baare mein daravani kahaniyan sune hain* (I have heard scary stories before about this lady Djinn). *Tum log itna jaano ki, tum logan lucky hai, bhaago jaldi; mujh par viswas karo, tumne djinn dekha hai - kyunki aaj Poornima hai* (you guys know this much that you guys are lucky, you have seen a djinn as today is full moon and energies are high)." He also said that, he has not seen a human in that area for more than 6 months, which gave an extra spine chill to the boys.

Pushing and shooing them away the old guard sent them off rushing. Ravi as directed went straight on the road ahead and reached an inhabited area sparsely crowded and stopped at a shop for tea. They could not believe they had sighted a Djinn, and the confirming fact was that there was a lot unusual about her and she exuded vibrant fragrance and energy.

As Ravi stopped narrating the above, there was a loud wild crackling from the campfire which gave all of us jitters and brought us to the moment! Ravi had googled later after the incident, to find many incidents in that area and nearby vicinity linking to Djinns and one of the stories clearly had described the djinn as an old gypsy woman.

Coming to the present, Ravi said that the ambiance, climate, and effect of the place had added to the encounter with the Djinn. We were all listening with rapt attention and excited to hear a new kind of supernatural character called the Djinn. Thereafter Ravi narrated what powers are commonly possessed by the Djinns and many more details about their existence and encounters.

It was already 1:00 am and few of the guys were feeling drowsy. So, slowly one after another everyone went to sleep, leaving myself, Ravi and Abhishek with the campfire. Just when I was thinking of calling it a night, I heard some commotion and the sounds of flapping wings a slight distance away towards the open. I glanced that way to see a dark something moving across; picking my torch I headed slowly to that direction.

On lighting the torch and waving across I saw four to five peacocks walking by searching for prey at this hour of the night. Shortly one of them let out a big cry typical of the colorful beauty! This cut through the silence of the night and caught the attention of everyone.

I walked back thinking to myself if there were a bear or leopard visit, it would be the cherry on the cake of camping in the wild. This might not be the case for others who were new and quite paranoid about such wildlife experiences. The cold of the night was growing stronger with a mild breeze in between. I thought to myself that chances of leopard visit were an extreme rarity as they are very wily and shy when it comes to a group of people, this was an info I gathered from the wildlife books by the legendary Jim Corbett and the kind. But nevertheless, bears could be a possibility as they are more curious and exploratory than shy.

I returned to the campfire to join Ravi and Abhishek; we finished off the last morsel of snack and drank some water before returning to our respective tents. The campfire had dwindled to a minimal flame and smoke (only one solid wood was left over).

Abhishek, Uday, Santosh and I were in one tent. The tent was a good Wildcraft tent and was very comfortable and convenient. We tripped into short conversations about the day before drifting into sleep all but myself and Abhishek. I was listening to the intermittent peacock calls and trying to count how many would be there; also, I could hear the wind picking up speed and gusting by. There were calls of some bird I could not decipher and in between the hoots of an owl. I was a huge fan of mindfulness meditation, so at this time with sleep hard to come by I was mindfully meditating on the sounds with my body totally relaxed and resting.

I sensed somebody moving and turned to the left to find Abhishek lifting his head and trying to listen in a bit of concern. I asked him the reason, to which he told, "Bro, I am really scared that I am hearing some things and it could be wild animals. This is my first camping trip and I am really worried if some bear or leopard will attack!" I laughed and reassured him that a tent is very safe and the animals would not barge in the tent and also that the fire is nearby so they will be wary of approaching, which was proven wrong a bit later. The fire died down and there was only smoke emanating. As time passed, I could sense some movement outside the tent which slowly stopped. I raised my head and saw Abhishek and Uday awake listening to the same commotion with rapt attention. Abhishek's face was perplexed and alarmed, the hanging decathlon lantern showed both of their faces in soft white light.

I asked them to keep very quiet lest we raise the curiosity of the intruder, if it were a bear. We kept hearing odd noises somewhere from the campfire side which was to the southeast side. The noises became loud enough for us to hear that it was from our plates left near the fire. Abhishek and Uday caught my hands and shoulders and asked what to do. I told them to calm down and that I would check.

Lowering the side ventilation of the tent, which was towards the side of the campfire, I saw that it was the backside of a black something of considerable size, helping itself to the leftover food. It turned around and scattered the remnants by which I clearly got that it was a sloth bear found in the southern part of India. I was totally taken aback considering this is the first time I had seen it outside of the zoo and that too, so close! The adventurer in me was enjoying at the same time the stereotypical me reared in the city, was also a bit paranoid as to what would unfold.

I signaled to both boys to maintain absolute silence and play dead; I switched off the lantern. A slight noise could bring the bear across to the tent to satisfy his curiosity for what was inside and also searching for more food.

Both the boys were not batting an eyelid, and I was watching through the small window like a slender loris in the dark. The bear got hold of a cover, tore it and started licking and relishing it. Then it kept searching for more food, eventually stopping when nothing more was there.

The peacocks were continuing as they were agitated by the bear's presence. The bear started to roll on the floor probably to remove the itching caused due to fleas. It was puffing as well in between in low volume, Abhishek and Uday came up to the window to get a glance. By this time Santosh also woke up and slowly sat beside Uday for his turn to see the beast.

We were all puzzled as to what would be the bear's next course of action! Just then it was disturbed by something and started looking around standing on its two feet, breathing mist which was clearly visible in the soft light of the moon. We lowered our position as if we were in a trench under the purview of an enemy army waiting in ambush. The bear was trying to sniff the air as they have a good sense of smell and started looking around. It could not locate anything significant, so it went back to what it was doing, the floor roll drill.

Bears have a very bad sense of sight, so we had less to worry about the tent visibility part. But after a while the bear started moving towards the tent as if curious to check it out. We were taken aback and lowered ourselves and went into a sleeping position with absolute stillness. Abhishek and others were obviously scared to their core, but I had no idea about the guys in the other tent. I hoped common sense prevailed even if they woke up, made no commotion or tried to ring me on the phone.

The bear slowly closed in and started walking around the tent. We could hear its breathing, puffing and the demeanor, it obviously was curious and searching. Abhishek raised his head and gestured to me as to what we would do. I could see profuse sweating on his forehead. I asked him to be silent and still. The walk of the bear to the other tent and back to the campfire area continued for a few times. It picked up a stick or something and started beating on the floor, I presume it was on the campfire as it did not like the fire much. It followed the antique by walking a bit further and pausing to look towards the other side of the road. It stood like that for over 3 minutes as if waiting for somebody, probably another bear!

*Indian sloth bear in the bushes*

We were all in the most heightened awareness and senses to detect even a slight change in the bear's demeanor or behavior, albeit none of us being an expert on wildlife. The only exception was me who had read a lot of Kenneth Anderson, Ullas Karanth books thereby having some good knowledge of the jungle and with some considerable experience in camping in the wild. The night was growing darker and noisier in terms of the cicadas and peacocks screaming in chorus. It was all adding onto the thrill of the moment and adventure. We waited in total patience taking turns to view through the tent window at the bear. The bear was strolling around with no particular agenda and testing our patience, the guys were getting frustrated as the sleep was totally disturbed and the bear was not showing any sign of leaving. Just then an idea clicked my mind, I opened the zipped door of the tent and picked up the stone kept there as weight and threw it in the air a bit far - aiming to make considerable noise. That was a brilliant idea, because not only was the noise loud but it also caused further noise by hitting something; the bear immediately got distracted, looked at the direction and ran towards that area, huffing and puffing loudly.

I signaled Ravi and he immediately got out - understanding my gesture, took out the lighter from his pocket, picked up the fuel can and opened it pouring the fuel onto the remaining wood and lit it in a jiffy. He picked a few twigs and a good log of wood lying nearby and placed it on the campfire expertly. The fire picked up quite nicely and showed bright yellow lighting around the area. Ravi looked in the direction where the bear ran, ensuring it was not coming back. He stayed put there to signal me in case it comes back. By this time, I quickly picked up the remaining food packets, putting them in the polythene cover nearby and rushed to the car to put it in the car's boot keeping an eye for Ravi's signal if any. This was a big risk, considering there could be more bears in the vicinity and also the one which vanished could make an express return.

Finishing this we hurried to the tent, got inside and looked towards the area where the bear ran off. There were no signs of the bear, sighing relief I looked at the sky to see the moon in the western sky which had a bright Venus for companionship and a star probably Sirius. I thought to myself, how wonderful nature is and celestial gazing in the lap of pristine nature without any of the city distractions or light pollution. I wanted to come more often for such camps and tryst with nature, but you know when you are in the corporate world so many factors are there which limit a traveler. I thought to myself, the idea of time and hurry was lost in this moment, because I was 100% deep in the moment and no other thoughts or worries were disturbing me. Time, be it clock time or psychological time, was no longer a dimension, giving me the pure experience of nature and the wild. I could cherish this moment as a precious one in my heart, the bliss of nature and true nightlife. How nice it would be if our regular lives could be enlivened by such moments and we live in transcendence to time.

Alas, I returned to the moment and settled inside the tent with others expecting to get some sleep. Ravi and I kept our vigil for some more time through the tent's transparent door. As there was no sign of the bear for half an hour, we all slid back to sweet sleep.

The inquisitive bear was gone for good but gave us a good amount of thrill and adventure before fading into the night. Next morning, I got up before sunrise and was a bit hesitant to get out of the tent. So, I waited for the Sun to rise and spread some shine before getting out to check the remains of the previous night. The campfire and wood were all burnt out and ashes strewn around; the food was also splattered around. The surroundings were pretty dewy, and the atmosphere was cool. The dawn was seeping into the morning with a lot of bird calls. I sat outside spreading my Yoga mat as the rocks were considerably cold.

None of the guys were awake, this gave me ample time to soak in to nature and do some mindfulness nature meditation. I chose the sense of sight and just sat looking at the static rocks and mountains ahead in complete tranquility; the scene was made dynamic by flying birds rendering a beautiful scenery of life in the early morning. There were calls of jungle fowl, drongos, bulbuls interspersed with peacock calls from a little afar. I just turned around to face the tents and the road and jungle beyond as it was from where the Sun was rising slowly. I just closed my eyes and immersed myself into the sounds around, mainly bird calls. What a beautiful feeling it was, for I am at a loss for words in describing the feeling of meditating on bird calls and nature sounds in the wild.

As I was meditating, Uday came out and shared what he thought about the experience of the night before. I had to come out of meditation and converse on the bear experience. It was his first experience of this kind in the wild and he was obviously over excited, the conversation was in Kannada and as we were speaking, we thought it would be better to wash the vessels in some water body nearby. So, we picked up the vessels in a cover and started walking to the road. Crossing the road, we walked to the jungle area on the other side which was sandy and full of shrubby trees. We saw some water and went searching for the source, which led us to a shallow jungle stream under a thick foliage on which the Sun was shining its yellow rays in all glory and reflecting back! I went down and sat beside the stream to wash my face with the cold pristine water. As I splashed it on the face a rush of endorphins flowed across my face to the head giving a blissful feel I can hardly articulate, thanks to nature. Just then Uday brought the utensils and suggested we wash the vessels using the thick sand as scrubber. That was an interesting idea and no better tool than the sand to wash the vessels as maggi, bread and egg had sticked onto all the main vessels.

We got busy scrubbing the vessels, making them shine without soap or detergent. Dish washing never felt so happy a chore and blissful until that moment. The Sun was shining bright yet mild on us, and we were thoroughly enjoying it. Just when a heavy flutter distracted us; looking to the right I saw a beautiful full-grown peacock fly and settle down to drink water.

The beauty was to see the Sun falling on the feathers and illuminating the blue and green hues of the peacock sparkling it with divine beauty! I can't ask for anything more surreally beautiful in bird watching than this gift of the moment. The peacock was oblivious to us and drinking water, probably because he was there near our camp the previous night. We observed it for some time and then got on with the dish washing. Putting all the vessels back in the cover and filling two bottles of water for the morning ablutions, we walked back.

As we reached the tent, a couple of boys were awake and basking in the Sun. We told them about the stream and to head there for water. And got busy with nature's calls and morning routine which are a lot different and interesting on a camping unlike our city homes. After some time, everyone woke up and went hunting for water.

Within an hour all were back in the camp and hungry like anything. We had a half bread packet, so I distributed a couple of breads and one banana to each and I asked them to eat slowly and mindfully so the hunger gets taken care of. We had brought a rugby ball with us, so that had to be used; but not before a session of Yoga under the mountains and sun.

Me, who was an international Yoga teacher, was not going to leave these boys without a session of Yoga! And the session turned out to be a real fun with the mild Sun, breeze and the open landscape behind adding onto the ambiance. Lot of corrections in *asanas*, jokes and fun filled the yoga time which followed with a rugby catch game. The fact that the rock on which we were playing was spread out in a large area made the game more interesting and frolic. After spending an hour, we wrapped it up and headed for the tent dismantling and packing. This was done in a jiffy by me, Uday and Santosh and we were ready for the next adventure of the morning.

*Rocky place where we camped*

It was time to say goodbye to the soulful camping spot and nature around, leaving with a lot of thrilling memories and conversations in the kitty. We could never forget the wildlife encounter and the moments which preceded and succeeded the bear incident. I did take a walk around where I threw the stone to distract the bear. Saving the stories in our memory registers for posterity, we hit the road and explored the villages ahead.

As we drove along, we noticed many groundnut farms around where people were separating groundnuts as part of the harvest. We spoke to them in native Kannada about the farming, harvest, wildlife around, the forest; and collected some groundnuts as snacks for the way back and slowly drove back to Bangalore with conversations about the time spent in wilderness and about Tumkur's historical places - bedazzling the drive. Looking forward to another thrilling camping trip in the near future we called it a day!

# THE ROGUE ELEPHANT OF CHUNCHI!

This story is about a wildlife adventure with a rogue elephant in a place called Chunchi Falls nestled near the Kanakapura area of Karnataka. The place is a good 100 km from Bangalore and 107 km from Mysore. Chunchi falls which I am going to talk about is a waterfall on the banks of the river Arkavati and is named after a tribal couple Chuncha and Chunchi. Tucked in the middle of rocky terrain and deciduous forest, the waterfall is quite popular for picnicking as a weekend destination.

The place is before Sangama, which is a confluence of three rivers namely Kaveri, Arkavathi and Lokapavani. It comes under Mandya district some distance after Kanakapura. About 3.5 kilometers downstream, Mekedatu is a place where river Kaveri flows through a deep and narrow gorge and is famous for its big waterfalls and rocky formations. These two are the must-visit places for those people who want to relax amidst pristine nature near Bangalore.

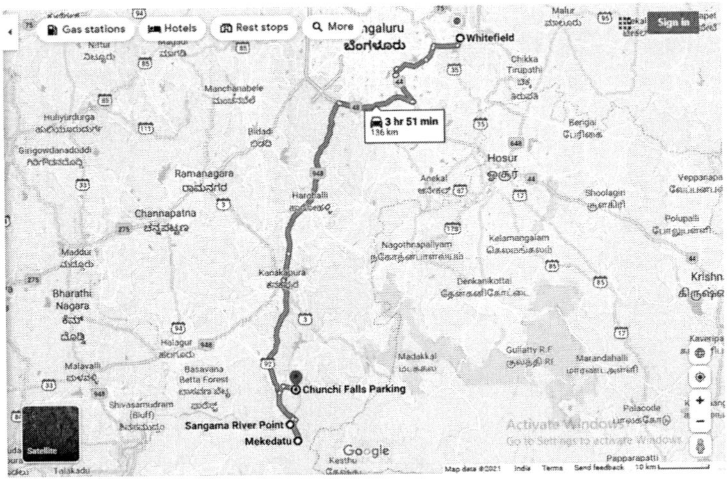


*Route map from Bangalore to Chunchi falls*

People who do not want much of a crowd, head to Chunchi Falls and the rest wanting grandeur head usually to Sangama as I noticed. Now, there is a deviation from the Kanakapura Road which one takes towards Chunchi falls. From this left deviation - marked by an arch, Chunchi Falls is a good 20 km through grasslands and fields. There are few houses interspersed between the fields and probably it is a village with very few inhabitants; however, near Chunchi Falls you have people living and doing farming as a livelihood albeit there being habitation of wildlife around.

Now I am going to narrate about myself and my good old friend Roshan's adventurous outing to Chunchi Falls around September of 2005 from Bangalore. It was a cold Saturday morning and Roshan was free and as we both were working in call centers back then, we had off on weekends. We had made this a ritual to head every weekend to an outskirt destination from Bangalore be it historical forts or forest rides to a destination. This time we thought we would head to Sangam falls on Kanakapura road not knowing that we would take a detour and go to Chunchi Falls instead.

Roshan chose to ride his TVS Victor as he was the well-versed owner and I parked my Pulsar 200 at his place. Starting from Bhoopasandra near Mekhri Circle we headed straight to Kanakapura Road at 6 am. We had to pass in front of the Art of Living Center followed by Harohalli and Jakkasandra to reach Kanakapura. The ride was a cool and interesting one with a couple of tea stops. Kanakapura Road has a lot of tourist attractions like Kabbaladurga mountain trek, Mekedatu, Sangama, Pyramid valley, Janapada Loka, Bheemeshwari river and Nature camp etc.

*Detailed map of Kanakapura area which adjoins Mandya*

The image above is of Kanakapura taluk in Ramnagara District and the main places of interest and fame nearby. You can see the famous places like Mandya (Sugar Capital of India), Srirangapatna (Mysore kingdom's fertile place with Sriranganatha temple), Somnathpur (with the famed ancient temple), Sivasamudram (India's first and largest hydel power project and waterfalls), Channapatna (famous for wooden toys), Ramanagara town (famed for Sholay movie shooting), Talakad (the famous sand dunes and the submerged ancient Panchalinga Shiva temples) etc.

So, as we were riding on the main road to Sangama through the Kanakapura-Sangama Road, we saw the state tourism board for Chunchi Falls, and I asked Roshan, "*Mama* illi hoganna?" (Bro, shall we go here?). He replied, "Of course, *maga*" and we turned the bike into the arch and entered the road to the falls. The ride of 5 km through the adjoining grasslands and villages was nothing short of exhilarating, the reason being the vastness of the open grasslands and the wind which was blowing. That short ride was a good starter before reaching the parking spot of Chunchi Falls. There were few tourists indicated by many bikes and a couple of cars parked. After this there was a walk of some distance to reach the falls.

*One side of Chunchi falls area and the forest around*

So, we got ourselves some tea from a small stall and started the brief walk discussing the prospect of the falls ahead. In a short while we were at the falls and although it did not look spellbinding, it was good enough with multiple falls all around and a good enough drop of 30 ft in the center. We walked towards an area where we could get down at least till knee deep. Just then a voice called from behind, "Nilrappa" translating to "Please stop guys!" We turned around to see a middle-aged man coming in with a concerned demeanor. He had a semi-thick, salt and pepper moustache, and medium hair on the head, and was stockily built with medium height. As he came near, I noticed he had light greyish eyes, sharp nose and a good smile. He blurted in a hurry, "This place is not safe, as there are some deep areas two meters ahead. That is also a spot where animals like elephants come for drinking water." We were taken aback yet interested at the prospect of animals which were never expected as it was completely a rocky area.

Then I asked him, "Anna, why did you come to us when there are so many people around; and why is this place dangerous?" He smiled, heaved a sigh and told me that a fortnight ago one visitor had gotten down and got sucked into the hole beneath and lost life. Furthermore, another guy was narrowly saved around the same period. All other areas including the drop and waterfalls area were safe. Roshan was all big smiles and gave a handshake to the guy and asked his name.

Nijalingappa is what he said his name was, and he was about to go when I thought he never asked for money, so he was not bluffing. After he walked a few steps, Roshan signaled me and I called, "Nijalingappa, *nil ri, el hogtha idheera?*" (Stop, where are you going Nijalingappa?). He turned back and told me that he had to go for some work and was on the way from his small hamlet through Chunchi Falls. I walked up and asked, "*Heli, illi aane baravaga alla andre bere prani baravaga nodu bodha?*" (Tell me, when elephants or other animals come here, can we see them?); to which he was a bit silent initially and then with a sudden enthusiasm said, "*Howdu nodabodu, aadre illalla, swalpa aakade allu neer idhe, mathe maradhu mele machan kettidivi*" (Yes, you can, but not here; a bit that side where there is also more water and there is a *machan* built on a tree).

This got me very interested despite being young, and this was one of our first adventures of the kind. Roshan called me to the side and told, "Bro, we can't stay overnight. I haven't informed anyone at home and neither have you!" I told him that we can call up home and let them know that the bikes broke down and we don't know if we would return today. He was not convinced but I pulled him to Nijalingappa and asked, "Tell me what's this *machan*?" He said that it was the name for the small log structure used to observe or watch the animals in the jungle, more or less a desi watchtower. I was more elated, as I had only read about it in adventure books by Jim Corbett and Ullas Karanth. Enthusiasm was very high among both of us, and we asked him almost in unison if he could set that up for us.

To this, his response was - "There is risk involved, as the elephants are unpredictable." We got butterflies in our stomachs as we were not experienced and got a bit shaky. Roshan said, "*Bandranna, nodanna*!" (Come brother, let's see!) Then he told us to finish off the bathing if there, at the other side where it was safe and not jump from the cliff if not experienced. He also hinted at having lunch and coming back by evening at 5.30 pm to go about the adventure.

So, with nothing better to do, we took a bath at the suggested place, a refreshing one, clicked a few pictures with an old point-and-shoot camera with delayed shutter speed, and then went to the parking area to check if any food was available. There was a fruit vendor selling pineapples, oranges and musambi; asking him to make a couple of juices and eating a bowl of fruits we decided to go to the main road to get some proper filling food. Roshan's big tummy needed at least a ton of food to stay sober till night!

After we got some rice from a shop on the highway, we came back riding all the way to the car park. But I must tell you that the ride was resplendent with brilliant views all around - courtesy of the golden hues of the Sun. The grasslands were all shining and were sparkling with the pre-dusk light and the beautiful breeze. Apparently, all the trees and long grasses seemed happy and singing odes to the skies.

We reached the parking lot around 5:45 dusk and walked towards the place the guy had indicated to us. The water was flowing rapidly among steep rocks as we walked further higher, the ground became hard, and trees were shorter yet dense. Large expanses of sky with nice cloud patterns like some doodles were visible. The parallel ranges of mountains to the right and left of us, as we walked southwards, corresponded respectively to the eastern and western banks of the water body. Now we observed that they seemed to be converging upon each other while the valley beside them narrowed to the proportions of a ravine.

Before dark Nijalingappa arrived and patted us on the back. He quipped that he came with some provisions, snacks, blankets, and miscellaneous things; this was clearly indicative that he was serious and enthusiastic about this whole thing and deserved a good fee for the same. He never demanded money but was thoroughly professional about the whole approach.

We started following him towards the place we were about to camp. A strong wind was flowing from north to south in the direction we were going. The foliage ahead was throbbing with life. Birds twittered all around, returning to their nests, probably at the end of the day.

There were macaque monkeys jumping from tree to tree in search of something, the breeze picked up pace and it was a great feeling walking along the river to the forest area. He quipped that we were just a couple of minutes away from the place. Shortly we reached the place which had a lot of trees and one of the trees facing the path we came in was a tree hideout. Something like a watchtower made of wooden logs and covered on top with dry long coconut tree leaves and dry grass. The observatory was perched a good 20 ft or so above the ground. And I was mighty excited and jubilant at the prospect of a tree house and sighting some animals.

Roshan was watching the sight with fascination when Nijalingappa patted him from behind and asked, "Lost in wonder! If you would have heard about the stories of wildlife encounters here, you would not dare this!" He chuckled and gave a good laugh, putting us in some concern. Then he said, "Oh, I am just joking, there's nothing to be scared off here, no tiger, just some elephants, wild boars and leopards that's all! And they don't attack as you think, rest assured." This was reassuring but at the same time, our confused and rookie minds did put out some anxiety and doubts, that had we taken the right decision. But some pleasantries exchanged after that, put everything to rest and we were munching on the groundnuts that he had brought for us.

Soon it became dark, and I got lost in a profound state of tranquility with the sound of the waterfall, birds and cicadas. It was a dream come true since college, as I had dreamt of camping in such a setup after seeing such adventures in travel magazines, especially outlook travelers and digests. Now here it was, and I was meditative even if I did not understand what meditation was way back then, beyond yourself, beyond the here and now, beyond everything. Just then Lingappa patted me from behind, yanking me out of eternity as I felt!

I and Roshan were enjoying the stillness and the languid beauty of the place least bothered about what's ahead or what we will have for dinner. We were expecting a small potion as food as we had not discussed that part with him, but Lingappa quipped, "What will you guys have for dinner?" We were not sure and exclaimed accordingly. Then he said, "Wait, let me show you something sirs" and opened his basket which was closed with a cloth. He opened it to our surprise to reveal a banquet – filled with fruits like bananas and guavas, rice and *sambar*, some *naati* chicken curry, vegetable dry dish and *holige* (sweet pancake made of jaggery, ghee and *chana* flour). As he displayed all these one by one, our mouths were watering like another waterfall emanated near the natural one. I for one, loved *holige* and we had twelve of them. Roshan being a foodie became so happy that he hugged Lingappa anna and exclaimed that, it was his best day in life. I was more than in the affirmative, as what more to ask for than a gastronomical delight in the middle of a forest adventure.

He asked if we would have the food now or a bit later. Roshan said, "Now, the food is warm; let's not wait for it to be cold." Lingappa had brought leaf plates, and we jumped in with all our enthusiasm of the 20s. Gorging on rice, chicken and veggie we ate slowly relishing and enjoying every bite and chew; satiating the taste buds and parched stomachs. All through he said that he had a feast at his house today as it was his nephew's after marriage function and there was sufficient food; but that he prepared the veggie separately as he did not know if we were veg or non-veg. He told me there are 50 more *holiges* at his home and he has to finish in 2 days. "You guys are tremendously lucky", he quipped and signaled us to the *holiges.*

Boy o boy, I was waiting for the *holige* all through. I took 3 and ate sumptuously so slow that Roshan was irritated, "how much time will you take mama?" I chuckled and helped myself with 2 more. That was the tastiest *holige* I had ever eaten, and we were thanking God, knowing that on each grain is written the eater's name (daane daane par likha hai khaane wale ka naam)! He had also brought 1 big bottle of water albeit we had our 2 mineral water bottles. There was nothing more to say, and we took the support of the tree and sat silently for some time enjoying the ambiance. The night began peacefully, save for the distance calls of nocturnal creatures. We could hear cicadas and crickets of all varieties chirping in different cadences. The single, shrill resonance of the plains-cicada is here mixed with the rising and falling sonority of the hill variety, smaller in size than its cousin of lower-lying areas but capable of emitting a far louder sound. The myriad crickets joined in the general vibration of insect vociferation, filling the air with the sound of throbbing omnipresent life!

All this while enjoying the warmth of the blankets which Lingappa brought, stories started flowing freely. But as the night deepened, something shifted in the forest. The once calm sounds turned into something heavier, a low rumbling that seemed to vibrate through the air. At first, we thought it was some branch that fell - but then we heard the unmistakable sound of branches snapping. The ground seemed to tremble beneath us. A little fear started to seep into us.

A wild elephant," whispered Lingappa in utter poise which clearly reflected that he was a seasoned local. He said, "They roam these parts for water, stay quiet please and do not move." But we both were paranoid considering if an elephant really wanted it could pull down our machan with ease.

We had not burnt any fire or lit any lights; the darkness was there but the moon had emitted sufficient light. When I gazed upwards, I felt the tree tops were lost in obscurity and the stars were visible here and there through the canopy of the leaves. Our talk a while ago was louder for any animal to pick up, and that was my worry at this point as elephants are sharp listeners and have a good sense of smell, especially humans. An instant later there came an earth-shaking 'Tri-aa-ank! Tri-aa-ank' – "the alarm cry of a frightened female", whispered Lingappa.

These huge creatures, as he later said, are unpredictable. "You can never say how they may react even under exactly similar circumstances, though with a wide experience of them in the wild, I can say that usually, under certain conditions, you may expect one of them to behave in this way or that."

After that alarm call, pandemonium reigned for a short time. Then followed a chorus of cries from all around us: 'Kakk! Kakk! Kakk! As mothers summoned their young peremptorily, accompanied by 'Quink! Quink! Quink!' as a dozen baby elephants hurried to shelter beneath their mothers' bellies. We could see all of this faintly and fairly due to the moonlight at a distance of about 100m.

What was more frightening was a prolonged roar from the water area now only a few yards in front of us. The elephants come here as it's convenient for them with a flat-water stream to feed from, which contributes to the falls further down. As water was sufficient this was an invitation for quenching their thirst. 'Ahha-a-a-ah! Ahha-a-a-ah!' A bull-elephant, in all probability the master of the herd, had heard the alarm signal of his mates; he cried his reassurance as he hurried to their aid, while another male, this time to our left but further off, also answered with a male roar. Then the first bull, coming headlong toward our machan, splashed through the shallow water. We heard the squelching as he hurried across the stream turning to his right, roaring all along. We were shaken and had our hearts in our mouths, when Lingappa told, "don't worry they can't see good." The bull elephant found the females and the babies further ahead and stopped as if to communicate his reassurance in silence. He lifted his trunk and patted on all the elephants one by one, which was an interesting sight. Then from the left of the group the other male who had roared joined the group, he had stopped roaring now.

Consider our mentally disturbed equilibrium, seeing all of this for the first time with fright and a sense of thrilling adventure, sitting stone still for a good amount of time. The herd started drinking water in a group. If either or both males bothered to smell the atmosphere probably, they could pick up our scent and start charging, but that was not to be. Instead, we heard crashing sounds which seemed to be receding behind us. The 'quicks' of the young had stopped. Evidently, they were going back to the jungle, but then suddenly the bull-elephant with somewhat long tuskers decided to turn back. His group went ahead and stopped, presumably for him to join. This guy took an about-turn and started coming back to the stream, crossing it he came further. Now he was less than 50 meters, and our hearts started pounding!

We could hear each other's heavy breathing; just when Lingappa nudged and muttered – "nidhana ussiraadu (breathe without making noise)". We silenced our breathings and were like owls with half closed eyes praying that the elephant would not notice us. The wind, which was silent till then, picked up a small breeze which disturbed Lingappa. The elephant stopped, turned left which was away from us and stood as a rock as if thinking something. Lingappa quipped in a whisper, "Gaali beestha idhe, namm side inda avan side ge hog bordu, devru kapadli ellarna (wind is blowing, let it not flow from our side to his side, may the Lord save us all)"!

Roshan was quite tense; he asked me what to do in sign language. I told him to be silent with a gesture. If we had some stone, we could throw one at the other side to distract the bull, but that was not to be. So, waiting in low profile was our only option. The tusker was turning from left to right and right to left as if a bit agitated. We waited perhaps fifteen seemingly long minutes to allow the bull to pass on, but both of our patience was wearing off. I shook the shoulder of Lingappa anna and asked him to do something. To which he signaled, he needed to think. Just then a breeze picked up blowing from behind us towards the stream, causing the leaves and branches to bend and cling against each other creating some unsought sounds. This breeze was unfortunate; we did not like it at all. Coming from behind it could spread our scent far and wide and warn any animals ahead. So, we prayed feverishly and crouched a bit, which unluckily broke one of the smaller wood bases of the machan causing substantial sound in the silence of the night. The elephant turned back, suddenly a stillness fell upon the jungle, a hush that could be felt as well as heard.

*The agressive Bull tusker*

To our dismay it started walking towards the machan side, it had sensed the human presence through the scent and was agitated and confused, although unsure exactly where we were. The elephant roared, which echoed through the tree, followed by the heavy thud of its massive steps.

We literally froze, I could see the death fright on Roshan's face and Lingappa was frightened as well if not equally. We knew any movement could give us away and trigger a deadly attack. The tree creaked ominously by the push of the elephant. It was close – too very close!

"Stay still" – hissed Lingappa again. "Don't make a sound."

The elephant had somehow sensed us and tried reaching its trunk up, brushing the base of the treehouse. The wood groaned under pressure, but the tree, seemingly an old one, held firm. The giant snorted, its breath hot and thunderous. Its eyes locked into the treehouse, filled with raw instinct, confused by the intrusion and presence of humans, its arch enemy!

Minutes felt like hours, we holding our breath could only watch as the bull elephant pawed the ground below us, its frustration palpable. But then, quickly as it had arrived, for some mysterious reason the elephant backed off, sensing that it was not going to win this battle for two reasons probably – one the tree was massive and too strong for uprooting, two it was not able to reach us enough to pull the machan down. The massive bull turned, slowly disappearing back into the jungle where the herd was standing, leaving only the lingering tension in the air.

As the last tremors of the ground faded, we let out a collective huge sigh of relief, our hearts racing in our chests.

"That… was too too close", whispered Roshan, still gripping the edge of the treehouse, his knuckles tired. I nodded, my eyes still scanning the dark forest ahead. "We were really lucky", quipped Lingappa with a sigh. "That was a reminder of how wild this place is although seemingly not. But now it is safe, no more problems boys!" To which we gave him a stare strong enough to burn someone. He patted us instantly to release the tension and said, "see boys, jungle is always unpredictable and quirky", in Kannada.

He gave us some water and a towel he had brought. We shared and gulped one liter of water in no time, and demanded the *holige*, to which he chuckled, and it was all fine now between us. We relished and finished off the *holiges* between us and relieved ourselves. Roshan wanted to pee, and Lingappa asked him to pee from atop on the rear side of the machan, as it was unsafe to climb down. Relieving himself, Roshan came back and wanted to know if there were dangers from Tigers or Leopards where we were camped.

To this Lingappa told, "there are no Tigers in this area, they are in Bandipur, Nagarhole area; what we have are leopards, but as we are a group it will not bother to trouble or track. So, be relaxed and know you are safe, as we are past the most dangerous creature of the forest – the elephant; we do not have any other animals that can trouble us. Enjoy the night awake or sleeping!"

We had the faintest of sleep disappear after the incident, and we wanted to keep watch at least as a vigil for some time. Sitting all alert for the next few hours gave us some good sightings. First of all, we saw a few foxes come for water which was an interesting sight as we had never seen a fox in the open jungle; it had a cream-orange shade (slightly could make it out in the moonlight) and is a small slender creature. I reminisced about all the stories of the fox which I heard in childhood from the Panchatantra and other tales. After a while we had some chitals coming to quench their thirst, this although a common sight in Indian jungles or roads, still gave us a happy feel as it still was wildlife.

This was followed by a considerable gap, so we discussed stories and funny incidents from our workplace which was an international call center. Lingappa was quite amused by the stories as he had never lived in the city or known such things in the corporate world, especially the fun in a call center. As we were conversing, Lingappa called us to show a jungle owlet perched on the adjacent tree branch. He switched his torch on and showed the tiny owlet in detail. It's a great bird to see which is nocturnal and a fierce hunter. At this point, Roshan asked Lingappa, if leopards (*huli* in Kannada) could be seen or if there was any chance that they might come.

Lingappa shot back, "Did you not have enough gentleman?" Roshan said with a grin, *"Athu ondu nodidre poorthi aaguthe."* (Seeing that one will complete the wish list.) Lingappa laughed and said, "I don't know, and I wish it does not come." We waited for the next three hours for some sightings but we could not get anymore sightings. By this time, it was nearing 3 am and the moon was well past the overhead position. Sleep was creeping in and we were all trying to stay awake.

Lingappa asked us to take a nap for a couple of hours and wake up by sunrise, so that if any animals came early in the morning, we could spot them.

We got up before 6 am. The night had been chilly and Lingappa's blankets definitely did a good job. We had a good sleep and were eager to see any animal coming by. Lingappa was already awake and alert. He greeted us with a 'good morning' and gave us black tea, which surprised us because we did not have firewood, or a fireplace. Roshan enquired, "*En anna, hege benki hachidri?* (Hey brother, how did you light the fire?)" Lingappa said that he went down and collected a few sticks and twigs, a few stones to keep the utensil on, and then made a small fire using his matchbox and had a small utensil in which he made the strong and tasty tea.

Now, tea is one of the greatest social drinks ever found on the face of the earth, especially in India; be it daytime or night, if we want to chill out, have conversations or take a break we have tea. This was a good way to start the morning conversations. Our machan which saved us due to its height and strength was hosting our morning conversations. We could observe the forest and waterfall, the place where the elephants and other animals came to drink water, much better in the light of dawn. The Sun came shortly thereafter and lit all the trees, the chirping of the birds and other fauna added to the music of the morning. We were wrapping up our adventure also by helping Lingappa fold and pack things.

We could not thank and hug him enough for the adventure and also saving our lives, on which he said – "as we do not have cameras let's keep all these memories up here in the head and meet sometime when you visit later. Come I will leave you till the parking area, and come back and take these things back to my place." We walked, sharing some fun moments till parking and departed, not before taking the phone number to reach him. We would not forget him for life for giving us the opportunity of a great adventure.

The ride back was pleasant in the early morning through the fields and pastures. We rode through the cold wind of the morning to hit back on the Bangalore highway and reached Bangalore in about 150 minutes. That was all - for one of the best trips with one of my best friends.

# LEOPARD VISIT AT THE HIGHEST ASIAN MONOLITH!

This adventure is about camping atop Asia's largest monolithic (single stone) mountain, situated in Karnataka, near Bangalore called Savandurga. This place is around 60 km west of Bangalore on the Magadi Road, and has an ecotourism spot in the foothills of the mountain. The hill rises to 1226 m above mean sea level and forms a part of the Deccan plateau. It consists of peninsular gneiss, granites, basic dykes, and laterites. Basically, they are twin stones but with a common base, one is called *Bili Gudda* and the other one *Kari Gudda* meaning white hillock and black hillock respectively. The age of the rocks is estimated to be 2-3 billion years.

*White & Black hillocks of Savandurga and Fort wall 1 where we camped*

It is incidentally located near the ISRO Chandrayaan mission monitoring center near Big Banyan tree off Mysore Road. There is a dense forest with a good road that one needs to tread, if you are reaching from Mysore Road; on the other hand, if you are going through the city and Magadi Road it's a 10-15 km extra distance through Magadi. Magadi was the capital of King Kempe Gowda the father of modern Bangalore in the 17th to 18th century and has a fort in Magadi, as well as another one on top of the Savandurga Hill. The name Savandurga is a modification of the name Savina Durga over time. Savina Durga meant a hill fort of death which resulted in the death knell of Kempe Gowda's enemies of the time*. It is also because of the steep incline and defense structure.

Savandurga has two temples at the base. Savandi Veerabhadraswamy temple and Sree Lakshmi Narasimhaswamy temple. They attract devotees from many parts of Karnataka. These temples date back to 1340 AD and are believed to have been built by the Hoysala rulers.

Another interesting fact is that Megalithic burial urns have been found in the area. Saavana in Sanskrit also means three-time rituals.

The place is rich with many varieties of flora and fauna. The hills are home to the endangered yellow-throated bulbuls and were once home to long-billed vultures and white-backed vultures. Other wildlife includes sloth bear and leopard. We had read about leopards in this area and were wary of it.

Surrounding the area is a state forest with scrub and dry deciduous forest covering 27 km. The degraded forest, which is considered as shrub and tree savanna of the Anogeissus–Chloroxylon–Acacia series is highly diverse, recording over 59 tree and 119 shrub species. Apart from this there are bamboo, peepal, fig, Champak and other trees, bushes etc.

The climbable hill is the white hill and the route lies ahead of the Narasimhaswamy temple, behind a few village houses. A few centuries ago, all this land around the hill was cultivated and densely populated, as this was the capital of the ruler Kempegowda. The ruins of quite a few temples, villages and forts are to be found around - many of them covered by jungle (where evidently civilization thrived in bygone days).

Now, let me come to how this trip materialized. Good friends Tom, myself and Kodandaram spontaneously decided to go camping on the weekend in August 2009. And I suggested Savandurga as a more than suitable spot in the wilderness on the rocky hill. It was mysterious yet with historic ambiance. Both of my friends obliged to the plan, and we called a few of our friends and started on our bikes from Bangalore on a Saturday afternoon. Kodandaram's best friend Faiz and a couple of his friends had tagged along as the ride was via Savandurga. Tom brought along his friend George as well.

The ride was a good one to reach the foothill of the destination by 5 pm, which was already late considering there was some climbing to be done. As soon as we reached it started to drizzle. We were prepared for this with raincoats and polythene covers for the bags. We picked up sticks and firewood for the overnight campfire all along. Climbing was not easy with the slippery rocks and a considerable ascent in front. We took away the shoes and started climbing on bare feet for more grip; but carrying the tent bags, personal bags and firewood was not easy on the way up.

Our initial plan was to climb full and camp just beneath the peak where there was horse stables made of granite 400 years ago, and there was a pond as well. But now the strategy had to be changed, so I gave the idea that there is a flat area in between where there is a small fortification protecting the area from gusty winds and also that there is a resting place made of stones, which soldiers used way back then. Still there was more than an hour's climb with a very steep climb in between, which we had to cover before it got dark.

Faiz and his friends, especially Faiz, was unsure if he wanted to climb with us and stay. A man of two minds always delays any plan or trip; the same thing happened here, Faiz kept switching from yes to no, albeit we trying to convince him to climb along. This ate up around 30 minutes of the time and finally we asked him to bugger off jokingly and started the climb at around 6 pm.

Now, within an hour the camping spot had to be reached - hiking on the slippery rock. An adventure in itself, myself, Tom, Kodandaram and a couple of friends hastily but in all enthusiasm started the climb amidst the beautiful view of the monolithic hill, the mesmerizing valley ahead and Magadi behind us. We managed to climb and reach the camping spot by around 7:15 pm with the help of mobile torches. There were a few stones which were kind of flat after the steep rocks, which we transcended to reach the fortified area which was surprisingly and conveniently flat and had a hard mud floor as part of the fortification. This was probably for the soldiers to rest and guard the fort ramparts, with a small shelter made of granite stone near to that. There were thorny shrubs all around and then after a few meters it was again the rocky ascend.

This was the perfect place for us to camp, as the tents could be put up and the pegs could be driven into the hard mud. Now, a strong breeze picked up telling us that the tent pitching was not as easy as it looked. We unpacked the bags fast and started pitching the tent beside the shelter so we could go in the shelter; but half way down pitching a strong wind blew the tent unearthing a couple of pegs. Luckily, I and Tom held onto the tent from flying off like a parachute into the valleys, letting the wind pass; and then 2 more guys joined to put the tent in place a few feet away. We put it in the protection and shade of the fort wall where it stood 4 feet tall, which kind of helped.

The wind was not lifting it off now. We drove the pegs into the ground amidst the pleasant and cool strong wind. Immediately Tom went and lit a fire in the pit ahead, kept there for collecting plastic waste; I collected the plastic waste and put it in a cover to carry down while going back (this was always my way of thanking the hill by cleaning the hills off the plastic waste).

Tom's friend just then suggested going ahead and cooking the food. But then we thought, let's dance a bit with the mobile music before proceeding to cook. So, one of us set all the items for cooking in the stone shelter and came to the tent. The next thirty minutes were full of unlimited fun, frolic and dance on the beautiful cold night. After a while, when our stomachs started crying, we pushed a couple of guys to the temporary kitchen and we continued the dancing unabated; since no matter how much noise we made it could not be heard anywhere near the foothills due to the elevation.

Ram (Kodandaram) and I went to the edge of the fort, which was the edge of the cliff as well, it was a steep drop from there on the right side. We sat there for some time observing the lights in Magadi town, what a beautiful view it was even though sparsely populated! The valleys below on either side stretched endlessly, a sea of darkness speckled with flickering village lights. There was light mist flowing by and that gave the entire ambiance a special feel.

Just then I turned and looked at the remaining half of the hill to climb, to see what the mountain in the dark was looking like. It was a partial silhouette in the light of the half-moon. The moon and a bright star-like thing, probably Venus, the evening star (as I know now), was on the opposite horizon pretty much above head. Looking back to the climb ahead the next morning, I could see the silhouette of a few trees and shrubs. I got lost in the view and the mild breeze that was flowing; Ram had gone and rejoined the dance. Casually gazing around I suddenly noticed a small figure on a hillock adjacent to the climb towards the monolith; it was unclear what it was, so I got down from the fort and walked towards the uphill. I went ahead, which nobody noticed, and I climbed and walked a bit till where the light was there, my vision of the view became much better. There was a small pond beside which I stood and observed the hillock on which I saw the figure, nothing was visible now. My curiosity did not allow me to come down, I wanted to check if it was any animal.

I sat there with visibility of the tent and my friends, as well as the hillock. After around 5 to 6 minutes, I saw the silhouette figure clearly come and stand at the edge looking towards the other side, and that was a bit frightening seeing its side profile. Now, I could feel it was some feline and this gave me jitters, but to affirm I took out the small wildcraft torch we hired with the tent; I pointed it at the figure and suddenly flashed it, and lo the eyes flickered back with amber shade in the darkness confirming it was a leopard. As I observed - its tail was also curvy and leopard-like (I have always been interested in leopards - the most elusive feline, and have read a lot about it). Immediately, I switched it off and sat still, to check if it made any movement or noticed me. As I thought, I realized that the pool beside which I was sitting was what it was looking at. It could be the leopard's drinking source at this time.

*Indian Panther or Leopard at night*

The figure remained still. Then Tom called me, and I could not voice my response for fear of being audible to the leopard. I remained quiet and slowly crawled down into a sitting position and started moving, not giving the hint of my presence. Reaching the tent, I saw everyone was cooking in the stone house. I called Tom and Ram near the tent and told them about the presence of the leopard, to which they were obviously shocked but only expressed it silently by keeping hand on the mouth and wide-open eyes. As we were all new to wildlife in the open and had never seen or dreamt of seeing a leopard other than in the zoo, we all were a bit anxious and paranoid. Tom went and told others to keep quiet and cook. Tom asked me to show him too, for he was quite curious, as he has always been.

We three slowly went crawling and sliding in the dark to see the prince of the jungle. In about three minutes, we reached the pool, and Tom caught my shoulder pointing towards the leopard and whispered, "Man! It really is a leopard. It is lying down so we can only see the head and shoulder hump; be quiet!" Ram was relaxed as always. He was known to be seemingly an emotionally placid guy. Tom asked me about the torch, at which Ram held my hand and told me not to take it. "Be silent and observe, let's see if it goes away," whispered Ram. We sat for a few minutes, just when the leopard let out a low guttural growl.

Silence wrapped around us like a suffocating shroud. We exchanged glances, eyes widening with alarm. Ram, the most experienced of us, whispered, "Did you hear that?" We riveted our eyes back to where a shadow moved - a graceful, sinuous shape. I quipped after a while, "It's gone guys, let's go back to the campfire and tent." Ram shot back, "Leopards always watch humans, even stalk most of the time; I have heard it's safe to be in a group and not to branch out alone."

"Leopards are ghosts of the wild, silent, invisible until they choose to be seen. And this one had chosen to be seen, we need to stay calm," I whispered. "No sudden movements. Let's keep the fire strong boys." We reached the campfire and kindled the fire making it strong with the sticks lying there. The fire roared higher, casting flickering shadows around us. Suddenly a snarl tore through the night, a sound so primal it froze the blood in mine and everyone's veins. All of us were now a bit skeptical of the stay near the tent.

I suggested, "Let's have our dinner and see if any more sounds or movements come up and then decide our further course of action." We silently had the MTR rice and rajma, veg pulao and the egg and chicken curry we had bought enroute (after heating it). The food was tasty and good, served hot with the pickle packets we had. We had a small discussion in muffled voices and then washed our hands and assembled in front of the tent, a view concealed by the fort remains. After the discussion we came to the conclusion that it would be safe to be in front of the tent and keep the campfire alive. Any wild animal is naturally scared of the fire, so it was a good option.

We got all the sleeping bags, mats and brought them in front of the tent. Ram said, "Let's have two people sleep inside when they want to, and the remaining can be outside with stones on the sleeping gear. So, we laid the mat on top of that sleeping bag and sat in front of the tent collecting big stones from the stone shelter. Everyone was outside because the anxiety was evident.

I fetched a few thorny bushes and cactus from the back of the stony shelter and placed it on the rocky path downhill which led to our area. Tom joined me and placed a few stones in a strewn manner to warn us if the leopard came down. All this while I was trying to see the silhouette or shadow where I saw it, but nothing was there; the leopard was evidently not in the vicinity, but our fear was definitely in our vicinity. It could have walked up towards the opposite incline where there was a big boulder with a cavy area to rest under (I remember this from my previous two climbs on Savandurga). Being ignorant about big cats in terms of knowledge and being young boys of around 25 years, we were doing whatever we could as per our common sense.

We both came back and joined the others. All were sitting with jackets around and warming to the campfire with due respect to the cold atop. Tom told, "*Beta log*, let's narrate some stories - interesting ones and keep awake for maximum time possible making it a night to remember!" George was in the affirmative and suggested horror stories. I rejected it saying that already the anxiety and tension is high, why would you increase it; to which Ram said, "Let's do that, it will keep us interested, awake and alert". Now the question was who was going to be the storyteller? Ram and Tom raised their hands. Tom won the chance due to his big foolish smile and insisting Ram to narrate after him. Tom started with a disclaimer, "Guys, these are real stories of the recent past from my life, and I am not responsible for your fear after hearing this" and then he let out a devilish grin!

I got up and kicked his butt, giving him a fun whack that he deserved. He started with a story about his own rented house in Indiranagar, Bangalore where he and four of his friends were staying as bachelors; all of them were Malayalees. Out of that, one guy named Pradeep had a separate room and worked night shifts, and was seldom available owing to his shift and sleep timings. So, they used to meet and talk to him occasionally. The other four guys were working in different companies and were always conversing in the non-shift timings. Now Tom and his friend Harish whom they called bear (*karadi* in Malayalam) owing to his body hair, had a doubt for a few days. That there was some kind of supernatural presence in the house, as three of them had had some eerie experience or the other and were somewhat worried. When they discussed this among themselves, it was more of a fun discussion to scare Prashanth who was another housemate.

This went on for a few days, before they decided to scare Pradeep with the same story and some antics. They walked into his room one morning post Pradeep's rest and told him that they wanted to discuss something seriously. Pradeep was a non-emotive guy, so he was cool; Tom started the narration about the incidents he and his friends observed over the past few weeks and articulated it animatedly to scare Pradeep. He listened to everything silently and calmly, and asked them what they were trying to imply. To this Tom replied, "Brother, there are ghosts in the house, and we are scared and want to change the house; its presence is there in your room too man". Pradeep was relaxed. He then asked, "Is that all? Or is there anything else?"

Tom and Harish were surprised as he did not even show the slightest fear or worry. They quipped, "Are you not afraid, bro?" Pradeep casually said, "I have been seeing this thing since my childhood, man! Yes, I too have noticed these things occasionally but didn't take it seriously." Then he dropped a bomb saying that he belonged to a family which relieves possessions and captures spirits, and that his father's main occupation was that, along with the *pooja* activities related to that! Tom and others were taken aback. Then Pradeep told them that there were not one or two, but three spirit entities there.

This sent chills down Tom's and Harish's spine, making them gulp the saliva in one go! So, the guys who went to scare Pradeep, who they had thought to be a timid guy - turned out to be a pro in this area, and scared the shit out of the boys. Further, he offered to ask his father to come down and scan the area, do the *pooja*, clear the house of entities and relieve them.

No one had expected this. Now their half belief of the ghosts or entities turned out to be full and concrete. For three days after this, all of them slept in the same room and were totally scared to go about the house even the bathroom. After a week, Pradeep's uncle came to perform the *pooja*, as his father was not able to come. He confirmed that the house indeed was inhabited by spirits of the people who died some time ago in the house. Uncle had exorcised it and captured all of them. They were to be taken in a *pooja* vessel sealed by *mantras* and to be arrested in a temple in Kerala.

After this incident everybody started respecting Pradeep and learnt not to read a person from the face value. Tom describes this experience as - "You guys might not believe it, but for us it was an unforgettable experience; and beware - we might have some spirits wandering here as well!"

We broke into a small laugh, George shot back "Probably the spirits of the soldiers of those times might be around and could be giving us company right now, he he he!" This lightened the mood and allowed everyone to ease out a bit. Ram quipped, "Guys, let's check out the leopard!" George accompanied him and took my torch along. They came in under ten minutes stating that they could not sense or see any whereabouts of the leopard. So, we thought it would be better to continue the stories with the condition that anyone who feels sleepy can go inside the tent and sleep for some time.

I looked above and saw that the sky was somewhat starlit now, and standing up I could hardly see any lights in the town. It was around 1 am, and we were here reveling in the adventure of camping atop a mountain infested with leopards. There was silence as Ram was thinking of a horror story to narrate from his life. I noticed that the air was crisp, carrying a mildly pleasant scent of some flowers on a nearby tree. The fire crackled, throwing our shadows onto the right-side fort wall. It struck me that tea would be a good option while Ram thought of the story. I called Tom and went to the rock shelter or mantapa to prepare some tea. I took the Lipton tea bags and some sugar, Tom brought the water from inside the tent, and we built a small fire on the small rocky stove there. Just to feel safe I said, "Tommy, I am going to throw a stone as far as I can see in the direction through which the leopard could come, is that fine?" Tom nodded, and I threw a considerably heavy stone in that direction, which landed with a thud and rolled on the rocky gradient making tens of sounds.

There was no commotion or sounds of any animal being heard. It was a good sign as far as our fears were concerned.

The tea was ready in a few minutes, and we took it to the tent area, serving it hot. I enquired if the story was ready and lo Ram was ready and waiting to start. Tom poured the teas to the plastic cups we brought and sat beside Ram. Patting on his back he told, "*Maga*, start your Karnataka horror story!" Everyone had their jackets zipped as the cold was biting into us at 1.30 am. I can never forget that night, rich with tents, mountains, historical fort, ghost stories, chilly breeze, threat of the leopard and tasty tea. I can say time had paused for the night and we delved into an eternal adventurous spirit, giving us one of the best serotonin richness I have ever known.

Ram had a story about a haunted hill fort called Jamalabad and vanishing travellers. The distant hoot of an owl punctuated the silence before the story started and the sounds of crickets was the background music now. Ram started narrating, "When we were in the second year of the engineering degree, we decided to go to a fort to spend the night, which was believed to be haunted; for proving that we four friends were courageous. This was an outcome of a tea session bet two days ago in Chikamagalur town with another set of friends." The wind seemed to stop now, and the insect sounds fell off - as if to say, please continue we are all ears.

Just then we heard a small noise, something of a scurrying sound. We stood up to investigate it, as the fear of the leopard was running in the brain even though in the background. Just going near the fort edge where there was a small pit, we stood there. We had put our food waste here, and Tom deduced that it could be a rodent. Everyone continued standing there for a minute looking around as if it was what we feared; sensing nothing else we went back to the story telling.

Ram continued his story of Jamalabad fort camping, giving us an overview of the fort. Jamalabad Fort is an old hilltop fortification on Killoor Road, Belthangady, Dakshina Kannada District, Karnataka, India. It is located in the Kudremukh range of hills, 8 km north of Beltangady town and 65 km from the city of Mangalore. It is also referred to locally as "Gadaikallu". The fort was built by Tipu Sultan in 1794 and named after his mother, Jamalabee. He decided to build a fort there, as he was impressed by the massive granite rock which was suitable for the construction of a strong fort. According to locals, it was built to serve as a watch tower to see things around when the enemy attacked. But since the British took over it; those in favor of Tipu were hurled down the edge to death. Since then, the fort has been abandoned and deserted. In the 20th century people started visiting for the view it offered and also because there were stories of curious people who went and stayed up on top, disappearing and never being found. This gave the fort a haunted fame and people were wary of going there after evening.

That's how Ram and his friends went there for the trek and stayed atop, to win the bet. The narration that followed was nothing extraordinary. The boys stayed atop, taking some food and warm clothes along with them. They were awake till 2 am on that adventure and everyone slept in the enclosure used in olden times. They woke up in the morning to a brilliant Sun, but no one felt any paranormal occurrence of any kind. So, they started celebrating the win of the bet and took pics with the film roll camera used back then in the 90s. They went back to Chikmagalur and got the bet money showing the pictures as all of them had returned back, to the disappointment of the rival boy's gang.

Ram said, "Haunted or not, but such horror stories are cooked up to prevent people from doing criminal or "anti-social" activities in such places. And that horror tag of Jamalabad fort did work out as people were afraid to go there owing to the paranormal gossip stories. As a matter of fact, majority forts in our country have a long and blood-stained history to tell, so these haunting stories become very authentic and easy to believe."

As we reached the end of this story it was about 2:30 am and we all were feeling a bit sleepy. So, Ram and I offered to stay awake and guard, asking others to sleep. We were awake till 4:30 am and discussed college stuff and stories. At 4:30 am, we woke up Tom and George and slept in the tent. Our nap was broken by Tom's wild laughter at around 6 am. I came out and enquired about the joke, and it was a trivial poor joke. I gave him a whack on the head and walked ahead.

I went scouting on the fort for a place where I could get a good view of the sunrise. Everyone was wide awake and ready to move on for the final climb. The dawn hit at around 6:45 a.m., the view of which was ethereal from where we stood. It appeared we could just jump out and take away a bit of the clouds!

Tom called me to wrap up the tents. We did the packing up of tents and stuff in 15 minutes and started the climb for the second part of the trek. The second part of the trek to the top of Biligudda was not very tough and we were there in around 30 minutes, where we could see a bigger pond and the stony stables for horses. "This could be a place for the leopard to rest," I thought. By this time, we had kind of forgotten the leopard incident and were enthusiastically climbing towards the peak where there was a small Nandi temple which we could see from the pond, as it was on the elevated rock straight opposite from where we stood.

After crossing, there was a walk, through big boulders, Champak trees and other varieties of trees. Flowers lay strewn from the Champak tree as if welcoming us with a flower laden path. There was fresh mist, and the ambiance was beautiful to walk through with some cold. Then we reached an area which was flat and covered with 5 ft tall grass. Our fears started returning if the leopard was waiting in ambush. Seeing the hesitation in walking, Ram brought a few pebbles and stones and started throwing from the adjacent rock onto the grass area. He threw and covered almost the entire area to ensure that no animal stayed put and ran away if a stone landed on it. Seeing no movement or presence he declared it was safe to walk through. We waded through the grass and reached the top of Savandurga - Biligudda in about 10 minutes. There was a small temple with a Nandi idol facing the valley and the viewpoint. The view and feel from this point with the mesmerizing breeze blowing across is nothing but magical and blissful. We stood there for quite some time soaking in the breeze and the scenery which is one of its kind in Karnataka, trust me!

Let me tell you something about the mountain breeze. It is one of the best soothers and emotional cleansers I have known as a mountain climber, in my 25 years of mountaineering experience. It can alleviate pain, dull mood, sadness and any emotional issues you may be undergoing in life. It cleanses like river Ganga, because the quality of the wind or air on top of a mountain is therapeutic, surreal and mystic. I can only attribute supernatural qualities to this air or as we say in India "Vayu deva's magic"! So, whenever you go to a mountain top, be there for at least 30 minutes to 1 hour and meditate; or at the least just watch nature from there. Trust me, it's super transformational.

We finished a delightful windy breakfast of bread, jam and peanut butter, and did some acrobatics and calisthenics, with a variety of boulders and broken big rocks, clicking some pictures along. Then we started the return journey after spending a good two hours atop.

On the climb down, I saw many cavy formations among the huge boulders, some different insect species, some uncommon birds and plenty of flowering varieties of flora. Counting the previous night's stories when we walked back through the touted place where the leopard stood, we clicked a few photos and discussed in detail the opinions of each one. My curiosity took me to the area around where the leopard was seen last night. Carefully examining, I found a fresh set of paw prints on the scanty loose sand near the rock on the left towards the southern side, everyone came running to examine it; meanwhile Ram went a bit further towards the other side, and then I heard "Ratheesh come here, look at this" – it was a relatively fresh set of poops, definitely not a dog poop for it was bigger and scattered. Inferring it to be the leopard's, we felt like wildlife experts studying poop. Apparently, there is a field of wildlife study dedicated to this called Scatology (Scatology or Coprology is the study of faeces. Scatological studies allow one to determine a wide range of biological information about a creature, including its diet and as a result, information like where it had been, its health and diseases (such as tapeworms), etc.

Resting in between, beneath the various natural shelters offered by boulders we knew that we were lucky that nothing untoward happened and that the wild had paid us a memorable visit.

We collected plastic enroute the climb down and had some fun, the climate also supporting with an overcast sky. The breeze also was a good companion on the way back. The only sad thing was that the trip was over; I would have liked to camp for two days there exploring each and every area near the mountains, which are said to have many caves worth exploring. But leaving it for another adventure, I walked along with the others quite quickly and reached the base of the mountain. We got some juice and fresh fruits as snacks and had a stomach full of it, before starting the return journeys on our respective bikes to reach Bangalore in a couple of hours. That was indeed an amazing tenting experience, giving us memories for life. Looking forward to another adventure, all of us returned to our corporate work life with reluctance but hope of more such trips across India.

*The earliest record of the name of the hill is from 1340 AD by Hoysala Ballala III from Madabalu where it is called Savandi. Another view is that the name originates from Samantadurga, attributed to Samantharaya, a governor under Ahchutaraya at Magadi, although there is no inscription confirming this. This was the secondary capital of the Magadi rulers, the famous ruler being Kempegowda as cited above. From 1638 to 1728. Mysore took over Savandurga, with the Dalavayi Devaraja controlling it from the palace at Nelapattana. In 1791 Lord Cornwallis captured it from Tipu Sultan's forces during the Third Anglo-Mysore War. Robert Home in his 'Select views in Mysore' (in 1794) shows distant views of the hill from Bangalore.

# Trapped Tiger of Chekkadi!

This is a recent story from my travelling sojourns in South India specifically north of Kerala. It speaks of a few days when I took a jungle retreat along with cycling in Wayanad. It was a retreat where I dived deep into Yoga, reading, meditation, wildlife safaris and forest foot exploration in the night. It was quite an eventful and adventurous four days spent exploring Wayanad, predominantly the side closer to Karnataka during the last month of 2024.

What I am going to narrate is the time I spent in Chekkadi where I stayed, after my two-day cycle or biking expedition in Wayanad with my dear friend Shanosh and his couple of friends.

On the first day we cycled from Kalpetta through Meppadi-Vaduvanchal-Pandalur and reached Devala. The route was very scenic and challenging as there were many uphill, but the destination, Devala is of great beauty blessed with tea plantations and pristine yet safe forest areas.

On the second day we started from my stay (in Thennal Jungle Camp) in Chekkadi accompanied by other cyclists from Wayanad Bikers Club and proceeded towards Byranakuppe in Karnataka past the Bavali border. One has to ride through fields, forests, the famous *Suku ettan's tea shop (this is the only shop which was open during the entire covid period and served amazing tea and breakfast, see pic below) and Kabini river to get to Bavali check post. At the check post, cyclists are mostly not allowed as it passes through forest areas into Karnataka, so we took the deviation just before the check post directly through farmlands and tribal settlements into Byranakuppe village in Karnataka. It's a magical place with so many farmlands amidst forests where elephants, wild boars, deer and tigers pay visit, most often in the night. So, they have tree *machans* set up to keep a watch and drive away these wild animals. We rode through the stretch crossing tribal villages and temples to enter the Karnataka Forest roads and circle back to Bavali through the check post; luckily, no one stopped us.

*Suku chettan's tea shop in Chekkadi*

After these two days I extended my stay in the nature-friendly Thennal Jungle camp, as it was close to the fields and forests and also that it boasted 145 species of birds within the resort area itself. The resort was having fewer crowds and had a pool as well. The highlight was that the back of the resort was pure jungle where elephants came every day and there were regular visits from deer, wild boar, and tigers occasionally!

On the first day that Shanosh and I stayed there, we decided to have dinner on the watch tower near the fence overlooking the forest, accompanied by our beers and conversations about the wildlife. The resort staff quickly obliged and set everything up on top of the watchtower, which was sitting in a sea of silence among the canopy of the jungle. As soon as we settled there, I could hear the nightjar with enchanting clarity, which was interspersed with silence and the sounds of cicadas in between. The wind slithered through the tree canopy, rustling their broad leaves like the murmurs of unseen spirits, adding eeriness to the entire ambiance.

We started our conversations on the probability and type of wildlife that could be around or nearby, having no idea that a big wild tusker came there every day in the night and also that a tiger was roaming the area till recently. Our solace was that the fences were electrocuted, and safety was promised by the staff.

We continued with our talks, which was the only sound at the moment. The night was intermittently alive with the hoot of an owl (the common one called *kalan kozhi* in Malayalam which is none other than the mottled wood owl). The call of the mottled wood owl is considered a bad omen by some Keralites. The call is said to sound like the Malayalam expression "*povaa-aa* (let us go)" and likened to calling upon the spirit world. In Malayalam, this species is therefore called *Kalan-kozhi* ('fowl of death').

Crickets chirped in a chaotic symphony after a while, and somewhere deep within the foliage beyond the fence, a deer let out a sharp, panicked bark-like call. It could be a sambar or a barking deer, as I felt. But this took us aback and brought in some alertness, and we stopped munching the snacks listening for further commotion, if any. It was followed by a deep silence as though nothing happened. The resort, though decently luxurious and very hospitable, felt vulnerable suddenly - a fragile island of habitation hemmed in by the primeval wild. A simple electric fence, a mere semblance of security, was all that separated us from the untamed wild that ruled these forests. Shanosh asked, "Cheta, scene aano? (Bro, is it something to worry about?)"

I did not reply and was all ears to any tiny movement, but nothing came by. We went to our chairs and finished our starters. The noise of the crickets was going on in low decibels, and I could spot a few glowworms making their way across the bamboo trees in the front. I pointed it out to Shanosh who had a big smile on his face seeing it, clearly indicating that it had been a while since he saw this beauty, just like me. Our discussion shifted towards this interesting topic for the next few minutes. And we wondered about the small creature and how it adds to the mystery of the forest. Their bioluminescence is definitely something we all wondered about and took a fascination to as children, have we not? As you grow up, the wonder in you dies eaten by the technological, EMI-stricken world; in spite of still not decoding this nature's secret. Think how strange it is to be indifferent to this nature's miracle, ignoring it as just another passing stuff. This is precisely why everyone should spend at least one week of a year in a jungle retreat.

Suddenly we heard a rumble from behind the fence; we thought it to be a deer moving towards the fields ahead of the resort. But the next rumble was a deep resonant rumble – the kind that didn't just reach the ears but vibrated through the watchtower.! We got up, leaned over and checked, the heart hammering. Beyond the fence where the jungle melted into shadows, something enormous shifted. A phantom of colossal proportions emerged from behind a big old tree. I grabbed my torch and flashed it, an elephant tusker with a clearly visible tusker! We were delighted yet shaken by the proximity of the elephant, albeit the electric fence being there to give us protection. The wild has a special air and aura around it, trust me!

The giant's silhouette was a monolith against the forest behind, his ivory spears glistening in the glow of the torch. His ears flared, catching the faintest sounds, his massive frame swaying with an unsettling grace. This was the most dangerous animal in the jungle in front of us, the most unpredictable and irritable kind.

The biggest strength of the elephant is its sharp sense of smell (capable of detecting water sources up to 20 km away.) Their nostrils are located at the tip of the trunk, for sensing and detection of movements. Their vision is not great they make up for it with the other senses. Elephants have good hearing, detecting sounds as low as 14 to 16 Hz (human low range: 20 Hz) and as high as 12,000 Hz. Also, elephants frequently use infrasonic sounds, which are sounds emitted below the human hearing range, in long-distance communication.

What has to be feared as a human when an elephant is near, is its vibrational sense. Elephants can detect human-generated seismic vibrations, even when such noise is mixed with elephant-generated vibrations.

Now, it was very clear that the elephant knew about our presence and position. But he also knew about the electricity in the fence, so he was indifferent to us. I made a faint whistling sound to test him; his ears flared, catching the faintest sounds, his massive frame swaying with an unsettling grace. Shanosh held my shoulders to tell me to stop it, as he was a bit frightened. But my best adventure with the elephant many years ago at Chunchi Falls, in Karnataka, came vividly to my mind and I was reminded of how the bull elephant then had given us a sleepless night on the edge. So, I was taunting this one just a bit. He touched the fence with a branch held in his trunk, the fence buzzed softly, a feeble deterrent against such an indomitable force. The tusker stepped closer, his colossal feet sinking into the damp earth with a muted thud. His trunk lifted, curling like a serpent, sniffing the air, searching for the presence as he could not see us. I breathed slowly and held my breath and signaled Shanosh to do the same.

The bull let out a low snort, warning us, pressing his weight forward. A chilling thought gripped me. If he charged, the fence would be nothing but a soft thing against his fury. The resort staff had warned us about rogue tuskers, about how they could dismantle entire structures if provoked. But now, standing merely a few feet away from this mountain of muscle and wrath, and seeing his power, understanding set in. We maintained silence and did not move for a while, waiting for the elephant to take action. For a few moments he was still, then in a movement both imperious and indifferent, he turned and let out a big trumpeting roar shrilling the silent night. I am sure the resort staff and farmers staying nearby might have heard it clearly, probably as a warning that a bull is nearby.

With a ponderous grace, he melted back into the jungle, his massive form swallowed by the dark. Within a few minutes, the resort staff came climbing the watchtower in a hurry. They enquired about the roar and if all was ok with us. We nodded, gesturing to them to sit with us, narrating what just happened. They were concerned and told never to respond or react to the animal calls and to be just silent observers. The fence may prevent wild cats and smaller animals, but a tusker is unpredictable with raw power. We took their advice and told them that we were going to come down to the restaurant for a black tea and then proceed to sleep.

They went down after ensuring the fence was intact, and we followed suit after a while with our things.

We went down and sat outside the restaurant in the open, under the trees and stars in the cool 20-degree climate. It was pleasantly cool with the moon showing out. We sipped our teas and told our travel stories, gazing at the starry sky beyond the canopy of leaves above our heads. We counted ourselves fortunate to be able to enjoy such jungle bliss, which so many of our fellow creatures, crowded in stuffy cities all over the world, have never or seldom experienced for even a day in all their monotonous lives. The cicadas were quite loud, and no other sounds were to be heard. But then, suddenly I heard the calls of probably a sambar or a deer; to affirm which we called the caretaker, Anaz. He waited a couple of minutes before he could also hear the calls; then he quipped that they were deer callings. He said, "Sir, obviously there are a lot of deer in the surroundings that come to have the rice grains before harvest, but this is an alarm call for sure."

Anaz went inside, called someone and came back. He said, "Sir, I called up the farmer sitting in the watch house something like a tree house but just 1 meter above the ground; he says that a tiger has been doing rounds intermittently since a week, so the calls are of the deer alarming other deer of the presence of the tiger. But don't you worry because it's common in this part, it's not a human attacker or a maneater, but just an ordinary tiger." But Shanosh said, "Anaz *bhai*, a tiger is a tiger whatever it may be or may not be!" Anaz and I laughed at this, and the thrill just shot up - 'we are in tiger country!'

*Indian Tiger*

I cannot describe enough the excitement when you know that dangerous and mystical wild animals are in the vicinity, but you are safe. Thennal Jungle camp was proving way more than our expectations. Anaz then said that he could take me birding in the morning through the fields and adjacent jungle, and that it's safe. He said that there were 155 bird species officially accounted for and listed in the resort property itself, and even more than that outside.

On asking if we would be interested in it, I was in double affirmative, whereas Shanosh was a bit doubtful as he had to go back the next morning. But I convinced him to do the bird watching and breakfast and then leave. The next morning, we got up early and got ready for the birding. We started with the resort area, which was a bit misty and extremely cold. We sighted many birds like the Malabar Barbet, the White-cheeked Barbet, the Orange Minivet (which is extremely beautiful), the Ashy Drongo, the Red-whislered Bulbul, the Oriental Magpie-Robin, Nilgiri Flowerpecker, the Racket-tailed Drongo, etc.

Now, about the Racket-tailed Drongo, this mini wonder can produce and mimic to perfection the legitimate calls of nearly two dozen other birds, including those of birds of prey like the crested serpent eagle, shikra, besra, white-eyed buzzard, and Oriental honey buzzard. It's a one-of-a-kind solo orchestra!

After some time of observation in the resort, we stepped outside through the side of the fence into the forest along the bridge that was connecting this part of the resort to the forest and fields on the other side. We passed through tribal areas where tribal children were playing and making merry in the early morning. Passing on, we saw the main areas where the elephants come for drinking water and the area which crosses across to the core forest area which is a part of the jeep safari by the forest department. Birding all along, walking across small ridges and mounds we saw a variety of birds like – Rufous Treepie, Crimson-backed Sunbird, Gray headed Bulbul, Southern Hill Myna, Malabar Whistling Thrush, Plum-headed Parakeet (which looks stunning in the early morning light), Malabar Starling, White-breasted Waterhen, Long-tailed Shrike, Paradise Flycatcher, Jungle Babbler (common one), Purple Sunbird, and a lot of other varieties which I don't exactly remember.

We were really loving the bird-watching activity, which I already had as my hobby way back home. But this just took the hobby further: one is the awareness of more species of birds among the swaying trees, which had a language of their own in the forest. Another is that I needed a better binocular than what I had back home. We were using a good Nikon one here. Slowly, after walking and exploring for an hour and a half we went back.

After finishing a short workout and a short swim, we sat for breakfast. Shanosh wanted to head back so that he could go to the office from Calicut in the afternoon. I tried convincing him to stay back for more exploration, but he would not budge owing to the shortage of leaves. Bidding him adieu after breakfast, I started pondering upon my plan. I booked a ticket two days later; to give me a total disconnect of two days from city life and also to allow me to explore the area further.

I told the caretaker, Anaz that I wanted to visit the watch tower the farmers used for keeping a watch on their fields from wild animals. And that I wanted a jeep safari through the forest the next day evening. This fixed two days of my evening activities; now for the mornings, he suggested I go visit the farmlands of a guy named Aji Chetan (Chetan means "big brother" in Malayalam) who was an indigenous tribal descendent and a wild tube farmer, saying that he would also take us into the tribal forest regions of Kuruva Island. The next morning, I planned to spend doing Yoga, meditation, and reading in the resort. Fixing activities for the next two days, I was eager for the adventures that awaited, knowing that risk was imminent.

I spend the rest of the day swimming, reading, meditating, and speaking to the caretakers about the property, property owners, the guests that usually visit, and the wildlife/birdlife around. It being an off-season and me being the only guest the two days after Shanosh left, enabled me to get the choicest food for lunch and dinner in an ultra-relaxed manner. Gastronomically, I was very happy having the sumptuous food and delicacies, that the only thing I wanted more was whetting my wildlife spotting appetite.

In the evening, myself and Anaz went for a small birding session in the resort and outside before the tea – sighting a few birds mentioned above and then an Indian Pitta, an Orange headed Thrush, an Indian Koel and an Indian Oriole as well. Finishing the birding for the evening taught me few things about life and the power of nature: first, it's a wonder and miracle that so many magical beings exist around us and that seeing is free, just requiring our attention and awareness; second, nature life can be so relaxed, soothing, satisfying and a learning experience that we seldom realize this for the lust to be in the rat race of city. The time in the open nature rich Wayanad gave me a connection to my naturalist self and the contentment which no luxury could provide me with. A valuable lesson the forests had was silence and its magical effect on the soul, as if some balm was being applied to all the wounds and bruises of regular life. I just wanted at that moment to disconnect from corporate life, bills, loans, EMIs and unnecessary obligatory stuff in life and take as many nature vacations as possible in this lifetime of mine with and without family both.

I sat after tea outside the restaurant under the trees, soaking in the breeze and listening to the bird songs. I can't explain the richness I felt with those moments with no hurry in my head. I meditated for some time and it was 7 pm. My psychological time now was ultra-slow and I could feel every passing moment as long as I wanted it to be; you could say I reached time dilation! By that time Anaz came out and called me to finish the dinner so we could go for the night *ghooming* (Indian word for strolling) and watch tower exploration.

I was a bit skeptical about the tiger stories I heard and enquired with Anaz if it wasn't too risky. Anaz said, "Sir, risk is always there in wildlife tourism, but let's hope that the short distance we cover does not lead to any encounters and I have a machete with me for defense in case." We set out thus into the night with a power torch each in our hands. The walk up to the first watchtower of a local tribe guy was nothing short of fast heartbeats and thrill, as it was pitch dark and we were walking through a wild animal-trodden area. Just then Anaz stopped me and asked me to look at the far end of the field where he had pointed his torch, I could see tens of eyes shining brightly – some moving and some still; he told, "Those are the deer waiting to jump into the field, when possible, to eat all the grains." I enquired, "Why would they eat grains?" He replied, "The grains just before the harvest are liquid inside with a white juice which eventually hardens into the rice we eat. So, when eaten in bulk, it gives a good, sweet taste and also a slight intoxication, which the animals like deer, elephants, peacocks and wild boars love to have."

I powered my torch and observed the deer, which were spread from the left end of a private estate to the rightmost end – 100s of them looking and waiting in eagerness for the bounty. We proceeded to the first watch house where a guy named Shaji was sitting with his bow for driving away the deer. He was dark skinned with medium height and of a normal frame. I enquired, "How are you, brother? And against which all animals are you guarding your farm?" He smiled an unalloyed pleasant one, showing the two dark teeth, but his grin was more honest than an ordinary city dweller, and said, "*Anna*, I am good and happy! The animals include elephants, deer, wild boars, tigers and sometimes peacocks." I latched onto the tiger and asked, "Did you see a tiger recently? Is this area infested with them? Isn't it dangerous?" My too many questions made him chuckle and say, "Yes, it's there, but not infested I would say, I just saw one three days ago through that stretch further ahead; it came two days in the night, I drove it away with this bow which acts as a catapult with the stone I use as an arrow. We are not allowed to harm the animals no matter what they do to our farms, else we will be charged with violating the wildlife act."

We were taken aback with the tiger's presence being mentioned. We saw that he had got even pointed wood and metal arrows for the worst-case scenarios, also the metallic cans for driving away elephants. His watch area, a small shack built 1 meter above the ground standing on wooden logs, was very cozy with blankets and essential stuff, as he had to guard all night long. We took stock of things and proceeded along the field edge to the next watch house of another farmer better known to Anaz. His name was Suresh, and he was a tall, middle-aged guy wearing a lungi and shirt. His watchhouse was a short distance away from the first guy's watch house and was better built with a height reaching 2 meters. We had to walk the long path as there were electric fences placed to ward off the deer and other animals. We walked through a small path leading to a ridge and reached his watchhouse after a small, beautiful stream. The night was already glistening with moonlight and stars. I felt extremely blissful and excited as we were approaching his house, to listen to the stories he had in his kitty.

He greeted us with a big smile and eagerness, which was not there with the first guy. This guy seemed to belong to a well-to-do family and financial background from the outset. His farm was roughly 4 acres and well protected with fences on all sides. He walked us to his watch house called Kaval Madam in Malayalam. It also seemed a nice place to sit guard, with blankets, a fireplace, a cooking stove and some weapons like the bow catapult, normal catapult, few arrows, and a sickle. Anaz introduced him and his properties around and said that he would be guarding all night long for the season of harvest.

He was a talkative man and listed all about the harvest season, wild animals raiding his farms, and how the police and state government hardly support them or don't give the right price for their farms produce and compensation in case of damage to crops. This talk went on for some time, and then I asked him, "brother why is your guard house tilted as if it may fall down?" He replied that it was an act of a herd of elephants which had passed through the farm and vandalized the structure the previous week, when they were not allowed to feed on the rice crops.

So, I asked him about the other wild animals, and he immediately lit his torch and showed me the biggest pests, which were deer standing from one end to the other in a periphery as if waiting for him to go, so that they could pounce and have their share of the season's bountiful delicacy. Then he said that Tigers do the rounds once in a while but are not much of a threat, as much as elephants, the nasty ones. The conversation continued between him and Anaz about a few wildlife and tiger incidents in the recent past in Wayanad while I sat in the watch house and soaked in the cold of the night and was enjoying this rare opportunity in the wilderness.

Around 45 minutes might have passed, and the farmer got a call where he seemed surprised yet concerned. He disconnected the phone, saying he would get someone to guard his field and come.

He kept the phone and asked Anaz to hold the torch and be guard for some time. "There is a Tiger reported as trapped in my other field behind the resort, I need to go check that!" This sent shivers down our spines, as what we were fearing was in a fenced field which he spoke of a while ago a small distance away. He asked me if I was interested in joining him; reluctantly I agreed. The adventurer in me wanted to go and the other logical part of my brain was unsure of how we would go there and if it was safe. That was put to rest when he told, that he would take the jeep from his house. I waited outside, meanwhile I observed the trees in the dark towering like sentinels housing the nocturnal birds which were rendering their nocturnal calls frequently. The air was thick with the scent of something strange which I could not figure out, probably something primal – the musk of the wild.

By this time, he got the jeep started and headed out. A little straight towards the south passing through a tribal area we took a right at the dead end shortly to join three other guys who were outside the fenced farm waiting for us. They had a couple of torches with them, and combined with our jeep headlight, it was enough light for investigation. They boarded the jeep soon and we took the jeep further ahead to observe what was the actual matter. On the way on enquiring they told, "a tiger is trapped inside the fence towards the back side and crying out, seems like a young one brother."

On reaching the side, we stopped the vehicle, switching off the vehicle and just pointing the headlights towards the side from where the cries were coming. We just got down from the jeep and switched on our torches towards the suspected area. What we saw was something very intriguing, surprising yet sad: a baby tiger of considerable growth had gotten stuck beneath the fence when trying to escape the fenced area. It was scared and letting out constant cries and panic roars, calling its mom probably. The question was, how did it get in? To solve this, we went to the only opening of the fence, which was at the front. The gate of the fence had almost closed from the inside and pushing it from inside would only lock it, so the tiger might have entered when it was partially open while trying to cross the fields; and once it entered in hurry the body might have pushed the door inside and causing it to rebound and close of its own accord. The tiger would have tried to escape from there, but the gate would not budge and the tiger was too young to figure it out. So, we opened the gates and took the jeep in the field via the mud road on the right side, stopping just before the area where the tiger was stuck. We adjusted our lights for maximum visibility.

The tiger was a bit afraid of seeing us and started letting out grunts and moans. Feeling pity, we wanted to help, but he was not too small to not cause harm, so we started thinking about how to get it out. Each had a different opinion, and one of the opinions was to go to the other side, and cut the fence using the cutter; but for that we had to fetch the cutter and go to the other side which was towards the forest, and there was the imminent danger of the mother tigress or father tiger who could come. So, we waited, not knowing what to do, just when there was a moan coming towards the fence, followed by *"oongh oongh"* which literally shook us.

Then, suddenly the jungle fell silent. The abrupt stillness was suffocating, unnatural. Even the wind seemed to hold its breath. We waited for a couple of minutes in ambush, and then, the sound of the dry leaves could be heard approaching. We strained our eyes toward the darkness beyond the fence and lighted the torches. Two glowing amber-colored eyes shined at us; it was the tigress which came looking for its offspring. Low to the ground, unwavering, staring straight at us from the thicket; it got irritated and angry the moment it saw us and let out a low growl rumbled from its throat - not a snarl of aggression, but a warning, sending chills down our spines.

I and the others exchanged nervous glances. The torchlight glistened off its striped coat. It was close, the fence was our only savior. Remember, a tigress trying to protect its cub is the most dangerous tiger in the jungle. The tigress took a few steps forward and came near the cub, which was letting out snarls of relief now that it saw its mother. The tigress was wary, not able to decide if we were enemies or harmless. After a few moments of keeping its stare on us, the tigress tried to grab the cub which was stuck in the gap between the fence and the ground. It tried to pull the cub out with one paw, but as the gap was less, it was unsuccessful.

*A depiction - but the tiger was just beyond the fence*

The tigress then tried to scrape the ground to remove the mud to create a bigger gap, but as the ground was hard it was a really hard ordeal. In between it also kept letting out loud warning snarls to keep us in check. For some moments we observed the relentless effort of the tigress to save its cub. But after an hour, we thought it wise to leave the place with the gate open, so if the tigress or cub wants to make use of it, let it do it. As trying to release the cub when the mother was around was too risky an option, we thought to come back the next day by break of dawn to check the situation.

The driver started the vehicle slowly; the noise of the ignition irritated the tigress, and it let out a few aggressive roars assuming we were going to charge.

Slowly the driver reversed the vehicle and we left the place towards the resort. Our farmer brother called people nearby and warned everyone not to go towards that side till at least the next afternoon, till he intimated them if it was safe to go around.

He dropped me off at the resort and told me that he would pick Anaz and drop him too. Soon after Anaz also was dropped, and as soon as he came to the restaurant area, I narrated the entire story to him and his wife. Both of them were very excited yet a bit paranoid as they were living there, and had to go out often to nearby areas. But Anaz pitched in stating that the event was normal, as this part of Wayanad was Tiger country and that was how it was there. So, concluding that we will get back to the spot as dawn breaks and check the status of the tiger cub we retired for sleep.

As soon as I reached my cottage, which was near the electric fence behind the cottage, I could hear some movement. I went to the window and stood for a few minutes; a tusker greeted me in the form of a loud trumpeting roar; it was feeding on the foliage.

*Indian Tusker*

I listened to the commotion for a few minutes and totally elated at the wildlife encounters of the day - the wildlife enthusiast that I was, went to sleep contented and connected to nature. Early in the morning we went to the farmer's house and accompanied him to the spot where the cub was trapped. To our surprise and relief, the tiger cub was no more there, and only a big pit was there beneath where it lay. "The mother tiger must have rescued it", said Suresh the farmer. "There is no other explanation", spoke Anaz. So, that was it – a beautiful and heart-warming rescue by a mother tiger; proving that be it humans or animals the mothers do whatever it takes to save their young ones.

We returned soon and I got ready and started my yoga and meditation, after which I recounted the incidents with the caretakers, bringing out more observations and finer points. My bus back to Cochin was in the night, so Anaz took me to the Kabini river and a small trek behind Kuruva island assisted by a local farmer called Aji Chetan. We then visited a few tribal area places in the human inhabited forest led by Aji Chetan under huge trees which were more than 300 years old. While showing a tribal temple, he took us to a spot where the erstwhile legendary King Pazhassi Raja used to conduct court during exile. The tribals were his warrior guards and he used to hatch war strategies against the enemy over there. That was indeed a beautiful tryst with history and historical trees. He was a good orator and narrated a few good stories about the place, people and history of Wayanad.

Then we went to his farm for lunch. There was a special rice variety from his farm called Gandashala rice which was being prepared for us. This rice variety was brought to Wayanad in Vijayanagara times by his ancestors when they migrated to Wayanad upon the decline and end of Vijayanagara dynasty rule in Karnataka. Ever since then this was cultivated for posterity's sake, albeit having a lesser yield compared to other varieties of rice.

The rice was naturally fragrant and tasty; I had a stomach full of it in the small hut in the big paddy field.

*Wayand fields and small hut to guard it*

Deciding to buy it, I enquired about it. The rice was a costly one and was available in his ancestral home a little far away. So, we went there and I bought the rice for home, along with touring his 350-year-old ancient house dating back to Vijayanagara period. I was totally happy knowing the fact that I got my favorite "Hampi Era" rice and returned to the resort after that meal. But I learnt a worthwhile lesson about the importance of farming, farmers and the rice we take for granted in the cities; it does not come easy, there is so much toil behind the cultivation and distribution. I can only say I am blessed to get the choicest of rice to eat in today's era and with my travels. I thank God and Mother Nature wholeheartedly.

In the night I boarded the bus back to Cochin to end an eventful and adventurous tour of Wayanad!

**Some trivia on Wayanad now:**

Wayanad is a district in the north-east of the Indian state of Kerala, with its administrative headquarters at the municipality of Kalpetta. It is the only plateau in Kerala. The Wayanad Plateau forms a continuation of the Mysore Plateau, the southern portion of the Deccan Plateau. It is set high in the Western Ghats with altitudes ranging from 700 to 2,100 meters. An area of 885.92 km2 in the district is forested. Wayanad has three municipal towns namely Kalpetta, Mananthavady and Sulthan Bathery. There are many indigenous tribes in this area, in fact the place is famous for Adivasi indigenous ancient tribes. The major tribal communities include Paniyas, Kurichiyas, and Kattunayakans, each with unique traditions and lifestyles.

The Kabini River, a tributary of the Kaveri River, originates at Wayanad. Wayanad district, along with the Chaliyar valley in the neighboring Nilambur in Malappuram district, is known for natural gold fields, which are also seen in other parts of the Nilgiri Biosphere Reserve. The Chaliyar river, which is the fourth longest river of Kerala, originates on the Wayanad plateau. The historically important Edakkal Caves as you all know are located in the Wayanad district; these are prehistoric caves with cave inscriptions dating back to 10000 BCE. The edicts found in another cave area of Ambukuthi Mala are evidence that habitation was also prevalent in the beginning of the New Age Civilization.

Wayanad district is bordered by Karnataka (Kodagu, Chamarajanagar, and Mysore districts) to the north and north-east, Tamil Nadu (Nilgiris district) to the south-east (it is the only district that shares border with both the neighboring states of Kerala), Malappuram to the south, Kozhikode to the south-west and Kannur to the north-west. Pulpally in Wayanad boasts the only Lava-Kusha temple in Kerala and Vythiri has the only mirror temple in Kerala, which is a Jain temple.

Now, let's come to my story of the wildlife adventure during my stay there in a place called Chekkadi. This place and two other places called Pancharakolli near Manathavady and Kaatikulam near

Thirunelli have been reported for constant tiger sightings and also attacks in 2024 and 2025. The Wayanad Forest Department have taken action against the touted maneaters, but have ignored other tiger encounters, as it's a common affair in Wayanad, where Tigers are plentiful, thanks to the Project Tiger campaign, which ran for years!

Before starting, let me tell you a lesser-known amazing fact about Wayanad forests. Wayanad is a mountainous place, which blesses it with a lot of Shola forests like in the Chembra and Banasura area for instance. Wayanad's Shola forests aren't just dense and ancient; they are alive in the truest sense! With the changing seasons, some trees shed leaves that glow red or golden, and certain fungi and flowers bloom only at night, making the landscape appear like it transforms overnight. This eerie, otherworldly transformation has led many to believe the jungle is enchanted!

Wayanad isn't just a forest place - it's a cultivation-dominant district, a tribal land, a historical place with many unfound treasures and also a realm of mysteries; where nature bends the rules, creatures vanish and reappear, and the line between reality and myth blurs. Those who wander into its depths may return with stories... or never return at all.

Wayanad's deep forests, stretching across the Western Ghats, are home to one of the most mysterious and elusive predators on Earth - the Bengal Tiger. Unlike their cousins in open grasslands, Wayanad's tigers are masters of camouflage, silently blending into the dense jungle, often watching you long before you sense their presence. This is what resulted in the many attacks recently where the human-wild thin line got obscured and incidents happened.

# Blue Sheep of the Himalayas!

Let me now take you to one of the most special places on earth – The Himalayas!

This story is from a camping expedition in the Himalayan region of Uttarakhand in Northern India. To be precise in the Tapovan-Nandanvan regions of Uttarkhand's Gangotri. There is just one word that comes to mind when I think of the place – White Paradise!

*The Great Himalayan mountains*

There is more than one reason for any enthusiast to go here. First is that it is the place where one of the Char

Dham temples called Gangotri is, next is that the origin of the most sacred river of the world called Ganga is from the Gangotri glacier situated in the deeper Tapovan area, third reason is that for a hiker or climber there are so many brilliant peaks like Bhagirathi 1, 2, 3, Mt. Meru, Vasuki Parvat, Mt, Shivling and so many other peaks. So, if you are a hiker, mountaineer, nature lover, or pilgrim, head here for all the adventurous reasons.

I woke up at sharp 4.30 am as I checked my watch for urination, and came out of my dormitory in Bhojbasaa, Gangotri. It was extremely chilly and cold, wrapping my blanket on top of the jacket. I went to the common toilet to be greeted with good morning by freezing water (no heater in ashram-based dorms). The kitchen was closed and the cook, staff had not woken up yet. I walked up beside the dorm to the front area where there was a microwave antenna and station. It was still very dark and slightly foggy. My sleep was almost gone as I had a good sleep, so I thought of sitting there with my thermals and shoes on.

Sitting on the veranda, I thought of the previous day's trek to reach this ashram. It was an interesting hike from Gangotri town after visiting the Gangotri Ganga Mata (Goddess) temple, through the pine trees and mountain overlooking the Bhagirathi River in the valley. I could see all the mountains of fame farther ahead like Bhagirathi 1, 2, and 3 along with other peaks. The sight was a spectacle to behold, yet one had to be careful owing to sliding rocks falling from the sandy slope on the left side. Walking the whole day, we reached the ashram for the dormitory stay given for 750 per head including morning breakfast. A raven called from nearby, with a yellow beak and dark furry feathers. The raven is very stocky over here in the Himalayas; they're the common crows here. Just then the cook rang the bell for morning tea, I jumped from the seat and ran to drink the warm beverage to heat the frozen body.

Black tea and boiled chana were given as a snack. Tourists staying in the ashram from different nationalities slowly started coming for the morning tea. Many were still coming to terms with the cold, especially South Indians and Australians. Finishing the tea, I went again to the front area to check the mountains, and lo behold at 5:15 am the sun had risen and was shining on the peak in front of the ashram. It was a delightful experience of the Sun shining its golden beams on the triangular pointed peak and rendering an aura of mystic pristine beauty! I just stood in awe as the peak was getting illuminated more and more with each moment.

I want to say one thing: if you are a human, start counting the sunrises and sunsets no matter where you live on earth and do not miss it if possible. After a few days you will realize that all these worldly things are transitory, and at least for a billion or more years the Sun and its light is eternal. Beauty will bathe you in its divine glory and wash your perceptions like no other natural phenomenon. Also, you will start to appreciate and enjoy your mortality. I am not kidding, try counting the sunrises and sunsets from tomorrow and see it for yourself. You can thank me via a message on social media!

Now, we had to start our trek by 7 am, so I went back to check if my friend Sandeep (my companion from Bangalore for the trek) and the people I met the previous night had woken up. They had woken up and were getting ready, so I also got into my trek gears and got ready and met Sandeep at the kitchen. Telling him I will be in the front garden area; I proceeded for a stroll. There I saw the Australian couple in our dorm Nick and Tina smoking, observing closely and from the smell I could find out that it was weed. On enquiry they said there are several porters and people who have it and will sell it to the tourists. Yes, it's an organic product and does not harm one if taken in mild quantities especially in a high mountain area; but still I would say intoxication is unnecessary and not needed when Nature can give you the greatest kick and high in its purest form. Man does have the ability to feel naturally high in nature without any substance, so why do substance intoxication. Anyway, it's my perspective, everyone has theirs.

Sandeep came shortly and Tenduk, our porter as well as guide, was also ready. Just then a guide walked in and informed us not to proceed to Tapovan as the glacier is broken and the route can't be determined. He lost his way and came half way back to Gomukh. So, he advised us to visit Gomukh and come back, also he warned us of the falling rocks near Gomukh.

Tenduk, my guide, listened to him in utter abandon and told us to start. I questioned him if it was possible, after all we had spent money and time to come till here. He said, "shaab aao me lekar jaega, inka mat suno" translates to "come sir I will take you, don't listen to them". But I was not convinced as Tenduk never exhibited that he was resourceful or knowledgeable. I spoke to three very beautiful ladies coming back from the Gomukh to the ashram. They were also of the opinion that it's dangerous due to 2 days of overnight heavy snowfall and the broken glacier, asking us to drop the plan and consider safety over adventure. Now I was in two minds, Sandeep and I discussed at length and thought of consulting another foreigner guy sitting ahead and tying his laces. He looked like a 60 something old yet fit man, with guide, porters along with him.

I went up and spoke to him, "Sir, are you going to Tapovan and if so, do you reckon it's possible and safe?" He looked at me in surprise, as if why this guy was worried so much. He shot back, "young friend, you have come to the mountains. What does it matter if it's safe or not; anyways adventure is risky, why not take a risk for a bigger adventure? I am going, you can join me if you want. It's my dream to camp overnight atop a world-famous glacier and here I am going to camp on top of Gangotri glacier." That gave me a shot in the arm and confidence; I told Tenduk and Sandeep, "let's go guys!"

We started immediately tagging along with the firangi, oh yes, his name was Geoff Wilkinson. As we walked the pebbles-boulder ridden path to Gomukh, Steve and his cavalry overtook us soon and were no were to be seen ahead. Even Tenduk was fast with the luggage he was carrying. I and Sandeep tried our best to catch those guys, but in vain; we discussed what they eat, how strong and agile they are! I was eating my energy bars and dry fruits enroute, and Sandeep was struggling with his flowing nose and headache due to altitude. By this time, we reached a clearing where the waters of Bhagirathi were flowing in all its glory and we had a small elevated area mound to sit viewing the beauty all around. I signaled Tenduk to stop and wait. Sandeep was having a profusely flowy nose and severe headache by now, he told me "Ratheesh I did practice a lot of pranayama before coming here to adjust to altitude but still, it's of no use".

I was rather pitiful of him and wanted to help but did not know how. We sat for a few minutes giving time for his headache to settle. He tried some relaxed deep breathing and lay down for some time. Starting after half an hour he was better; in another half an hour we reached Gomukh, the official origin of Bhagirathi or main source of Ganga. It was as if I could say a pure heavenly feeling, with a 360 degree view all around. The mouth of the Ganges called Gomukh in front which was part of the Gangotri glacier, this glacier was till the ashram 4 km away 50 years back and till the Gangotri town Suryakund waterfall 200 years ago. Just imagine how much it has receded in the past many years, that just shows that climate change and that glacier melting is real my friends.

*Bhagirathi Peaks in morning*

We could see a few small peaks behind us and the Bhagirathi peaks on the left side. The famous mount Meru was in front which had never been successfully summited till then as was a little portion of mount Shivling visible from there (Shivling is also not summited till date). The glacier formed a "U" formation and Gomukh was exactly like the mouth of a cow as its nomenclature goes. Behind us there were sandy and rocky hillocks which were throwing rocks of many sizes constantly at frequent intervals and Tenduk warned us to keep an eye out and be careful. I was sitting a little afar and enjoying the view around with Tenduk. Sandeep in his enthusiasm not heeding to the warning went near Gomukh to view it up close and take photos.

He took one photo and then we heard a thud sound and looked to the left to see him dodge falling rocks, narrowly missing a considerably big rock hitting him until he reached where we sat. He was panting and his heartbeat was high, no wonder considering he just escaped death or a serious injury. It was unbelievable, as if the rocks were waiting for him till then to slide and fall where he was standing. Thanking all gods for saving his life, he said sorry to Tenduk and me. Tenduk, as calm as ever, said, "brother I told you it's dangerous". That was the end of my adventure there. I went and washed my face in the Gomukh water in front, knowing definitely for sure that it can't be polluted as it was originating from the glacier in front of me. I also collected the purest Ganga water in a small bottle for home, as per Hindus' traditional custom and reverence of Ganga.

Tenduk said that we had to reach Tapovan before the Sun was gone owing to the overcast climate. He also indicated that a snowfall was imminent. I jumped up ready to go, but Sandeep did not. I asked him about his lack of interest and he said that he was not feeling very well and did not want to risk his health. "I still have a severe headache, a nose flowing like a stream and some amount of nausea Ratheesh, you guys carry on; I will rest and wait in the ashram for the day".

I took pity on Sandeep as he was very enthusiastic about Tapovan and had done a lot of research. Nevertheless, I proceeded with Tenduk wading through the rocks to reach the Gangotri glacier.

Now was the tricky part, there were crevasses on both sides and there was a narrow ridge of considerable length I had to cross trusting the ice to reach the other side leading up to the climb of Tapovan. My shoes from Decathlon had to go through the test of grip in this challenging situation. Taking a long breath, I walked carefully hoping the snow did not give up on the ridge. A fall would definitely injure me and also take some rescue effort from Tenduk in taking me out, considering there was hardly anyone going to Tapovan. Everyone was satisfied with Gomukh and going back to base camp ashram during the rough weather condition.

I took deep long breaths, concentrated on the ridge and slowly made it to the other side successfully. This was my first trip on glacier and snow, and that too on the glacier on top of Gomukh. Crossing it was special, but now remained the bigger challenge of getting to Tapovan when the route was decimated by snowfall. I asked Tenduk of the feasibility, and he was grinning saying, "come on shaab, I will take you safely!" That was a viral confidence, and I proceeded on raw ice and snow behind him. The climb was a steep uphill and I had to stop every minute to gasp for breath for around 30 seconds at least. I climbed this way behind him on the mud path, always afraid - if it slips, I will be down lying on the glacier. The arduous climb went on for 30 min, then we reached a beautiful waterfall coming down from Tapovan, it was quite a sight.

I had to take few photos with the majestic Shivling Mountain in the background using my high-end point & shoot camera before crossing the waterfall, the photo frame was exactly like a Shivlinga in temple; the water stream going across the Shivling peak and falling on the right as we have it on the deity linga. It was mesmerizing to see that sight and behold it. I requested Tenduk for a few minutes and sat there soaking it all in during my 5 min meditation, then got up and proceeded.

As soon as we crossed the waterfall it started snowing suddenly. I put on my poncho and strode along with Tenduk to reach the top of Tapovan. On the left was a stream which led to the waterfall and in front were the mountains and Tapovan peak was covered with mist. There was hardly any visibility owing to the mist all around. Meanwhile the snowing stopped and the atmosphere turned very chilly. We stopped there for me to take a few snaps of the 360-degree sight all around albeit only a few mountains were visible on the right.

A few minutes later the veil of mist cleared right in front of our eyes to reveal the divine Shivling peak, as if revealing a secret vantage by unveiling a curtain. I can only say that this was one of the most mesmerizing sights I ever witnessed of a mountain and meadow. The Shivling was covered with snow and there was a small round of mist on top of it, giving it a divine look and feel. I could see grass and meadows all around. There could be more than 500 tents pitched atop that area, at the foothill of mt. Shivling.

*Misty Tapovan and Shivling peak in background*

Tenduk started showing me around. There was a small pond on the left side, kind of very beautiful. And there was this stream flowing from Shivling Mountain through the meadow. There were a couple of small bridges to cross to the other side where Tenduk told me few Saddhus and Babas were staying. We went ahead to see a small house covered in snow; you could call it an elaborate hut. Tenduk educated me that it belonged to a baba called Mouni baba. He spoke for only six months and was in complete silence for the other half of the year. This was repeated year after year, but he hosted guests with a spiritual inclination after scrutinizing the tourist. There were basic facilities like mat and blankets along with food and black tea. I saw two foreign ladies going around the cottage with their guide to ascertain if they could stay there. We went and sat on the chair in front of the cottage. I clicked a few snaps from the site ahead and the cottage.

*Mouni baba ashram and dormitory*

Just then the baba came out, he was of a wiry frame with long black beard, dressed in black and saffron colored clothes. He had a black sun glass and a long sharp nose. He started smiling at us and queried Tenduk about us in sign language. Tenduk answered that we were hikers and wanted to camp there. He grinned as if he knew that, and enquired with hands if we needed to stay in his cottage; to which I promptly said no. He requested us to stay further and asked us to look inside, but I was reluctant, which did not go well with him. I was getting a gut feel that this guy is an outright fraud and rascal staying atop with all amenities to lure foreigners into staying there and make good money out of it. But as we got up to leave, he asked us to have some black tea. Tenduk asked me to sit, and we took the tea; the guest who brought it also gave us chapatis.

As we sat sipping the tea, I asked the baba if I could take a photo of him. He said no, I requested him again. He smiled again and obliged, but to my surprise the camera did not work; the lens got stuck and would not budge. Outright strange because it was working just a moment before and never had a problem till then. I tried my best and kept fiddling with it in a bit of tension, as it was my first cam, and the motor seemed to be jammed and unyielding front or back.

I looked at Tenduk and then the baba. Baba asked me if the cam was not working, with a wicked smile. I nodded and said it was working a moment before, and it was totally stuck now. He asked us to leave immediately, with a sudden shift in his hospitality. I got offended, but had to leave as we had to leave either way. I was confused and got down the steps of the cottage and kept trying my luck with the cam. Suddenly it started working, as if it had no issues ever; I tried a few more times switching it on and off, but the motor did not seem to have any issues. I asked Tenduk, "How's that possible, did the baba do any magic? Tenduk scratched his head and said, "ho shaktha hai shaab (it could be sir)". He told me that people believe that the baba has some powers as he has been meditating and keeping maun vrat (vow of silence) for a long time.

As we walked through the snow, I was pondering if it could really be the case! I had heard about babas who can do small as well as big miracles in the Himalayas. In a book called "Living with the Himalayan Masters" by Swami Rama, he cites a lot of these miracles of sadhus.

But here I had a real time incident, and I didn't know if it was a coincidence of the electronic glitch or a real-time mind power of baba. But then, fast forward: the camera never gave me a similar issue for months and years even after I was back, and I have used this camera later in other cold expeditions as well, and it has performed really well. So, the story of the mouni baba incident stayed as a strange mystery, because he thought we would stay there after accepting his food and hospitality, but we did not. I do not know if he has any tantric practices in the night, where he involves the guests! And there are babas as I have heard from mountaineers/ hikers of the Himalayas who have some powers but are lost to petty ego trips and displays. So, putting that at the back of my mind, I crossed the small bridge and went to the meadow.

*Camping area in Tapovan and blue pond beside it*

We saw a tent being pitched and walked towards it. I went near and saw that Geoff was sitting inside and having sandwiches! He was pleasantly surprised and offered me a sandwich. I took it quickly as I was famished after the climb and we had no ready-made food. Geoff kind of looked like yesteryear Hollywood star Harrison Ford and was a fit man. He told me that it was his dream to stay atop one of the most beautiful glaciers and watch the moon in the night. And it was a full moon night that day. Geoff also had support staff and a kitchen tent pitched for his overnight stay and the next day.

We spoke at length of how we dodged the bad climate and broken glacier to reach there and the plans for the evening. He invited me to pitch our tent beside his, to which I was reluctant. I told him that I will pitch it a little far to have that special experience of solitude atop a great campsite like the mt. Shivling. I ate two sandwiches and gave one to Tenduk, and asked Tenduk to pitch our tent a little away towards Shivling's snow base. I continued conversing with Geoff about his life.

Geoff was an architect constructing green homes for the public till a couple of years ago, for two years he retired and sold his house and moved to Colorado with a friend. He just had one water-raft and the rest of his money in a savings account for travelling the world. He started his globetrotting a couple of years back and had covered cheap countries in Africa and southeast Asia before coming to India for a 6-month trip. On enquiry if he was married, he told me that he almost got married two times but both got cancelled in strange ways, after which he decided to stay single and enjoy life. He was an expert rafter on the Colorado river and had a sufficient bank balance to enable him to travel for at least 10 years. I questioned him if he would deny that he is a rich millionaire, to which he laughed for a while and said that you need to be smart rather than rich to travel the world. Yes, money is needed but not an infinite amount, rather a finite amount to make you enjoy each experience in a country to the fullest.

Just then we saw a few people making their way towards our camping area. As they approached, I saw that they were the same two ladies whom we had at breakfast in Gangotri town. One was a US settled Israeli named Gabriella and was a physiotherapist, the other was a South American named Bella from Argentina settled in the US, working as an academic admin. The best part was both were very beautiful especially the Israeli lady and they were fun. As they came near, they recognized me and were very happy to see me. We greeted each other with a good long hug as if we were friends for life. They had their support staff of porters, guides and cooks as well. I thought that in the absence of a kitchen and cook I could get some food from both the tent kitchens, for we had only a few chapati rolls packed for food. That was a pleasant gastronomic thought to leave me relaxed.

I took a short leave from them, as they had to pitch their tent and I had to check if Tenduk had pitched ours. I walked and reached my tent, a single one and Tenduk had his pitch a few meters from mine. I was very happy at last to do my first camping atop deep Himalayan peaks. I took a rest for an hour and freshened myself before going to Geoff and Gabriella's tents. Geoff was reading a book as it was sunny outside and pleasantly cool inside of the tent. His kitchen was probably making tea as I could see steam flowing above his tent kitchen. I greeted him good evening and sat a brief moment outside enquiring his plans for the evening and next morning. He wanted to do an extended walk in the evening exploring the area and then put some music on his Bluetooth speaker and enjoy his night with the food. And next morning he wanted to do some yoga and try a bath in the stream before exploring the mountains around and then pack by afternoon. I was expecting the tea to come, but as he was busy reading and the tea did not show up; I took leave and proceeded to Gabriella's tent.

Both the ladies were sitting on their sleeping bags in jackets and conversing to glory, when I greeted them. They were very welcoming and gave me a seat inside their big tent, well-lit with some lights. They just finished a smoke and offered me one, which I refused as I was not into smoking or had the slightest inclination. Gabriella asked about my whereabouts, and was very interested to know about Bangalore where I came from and the IT industry over there. Bella was all ears being a good enthusiastic listener. I told them about my life in Bangalore, busy with work, bicycling, Yoga, trekking, photography, mountaineering occasionally and gym. I told them that I do host photography exhibitions in many art galleries in Bangalore, to which they took great liking. Then the next half hour was in depth conversation about photography, its nuances and how that can bring out the creative side of a person, enable travel and provide much joy.

Gabriella had a Nikon P&S and was an enthusiastic travel and street photographer although just a rookie as she claimed. Just then I asked if she had the Nikon camera right there, she nodded and took it from her backpack and handed over to me. I asked them to peep out of the tent, and that I would click a funny yet memorable photo for them. They were excited and were ready for posing; I asked them to peep out when I said, with wild funny expressions one beside other and change the expressions and stance four to five times. I put the camera in manual mode got a high shutter value and a low aperture for fast candid capture.

On my signal they did what I told and the shutter clicked multiple times. The tent with the ladies had the snow-clad mountain as the background, and the meadow as an ambiance. I ran and showed them the result where five pictures were taken in different angles one after another capturing the expressions and the composition being super awesome. Both ladies jumped in excitement as the photos transcended whatever expectations they had and were well lit, capturing the mountains, meadows and a few Himalayan blue sheep also grazing in the background. It was like print perfect and they commended me about the composition which I always knew was my strength. They were all giggles and we had some good fun clicking more photos with the ladies taking all kinds of poses. By this time Geoff joined us and he suggested a walk to explore the mountainous region. We all were interested and ready.

So, we proceeded along the front of Shivling peak along the stream. As we walked, half the stream was frozen with ice sheets, the other half flowed unabatedly creating a soft music. Geoff paired with Bella and I joined Gabriella strolling at slow pace. We saw few Bharals or Himalayan blue sheep in a herd grazing a short distance away. Gabriella wanted a close pic, so we went closer to click some pics of the Bharals. We asked Geoff to continue and proceeded slowly so as not to scare the blue sheep. As we neared, I took the camera from Gabriella and started clicking, Gabriella held my shoulder as the size of the Bharals was a bit of a concern considering they had these considerably big and seemingly strong horns.

As I continued the clicks at different exposures and zooms, one of the Bharal heard the click and started staring at us. It started sniffing hard and the other Bharals also became aware, now it was a bit tricky as we had the stream behind us and the Bharals had a downhill to charge at us if they did. Gabriella asked, "Rath, do you reckon they would charge?" I replied, "I don't know, but let's be ready in case". She held my hand tightly; we stood still for a few moments. The Bharals were usually very defensive as the porters had told us early, so we had to be extra careful. I looked behind and saw that there was a rock behind us on the left side probably less than 100 feet away. I told Gabriella in a whisper, we may have to run to that if charged, I put the camera around my neck and held her hand tightly. Just then Geoff, unaware of this, called us from behind and the Bharals got alert. Suddenly in the wink of an eye they charged at us as a herd. My heart came to my mouth, but I pulled Gabriella and started running for the rock.

I ran probably the fastest in my life and my friend was equally fast. We reached the rock, and I climbed quickly as I was versed with bouldering. Gabriella was struggling, so I gave her a hand and pulled her up in a swift movement. The Bharals came rushing, bending their head to butt us off, and got furious seeing us on top of the boulder and safe. They waited sniffing in exasperation, for us to come down. I quickly called out to Geoff and asked him to drive this herd away. Gabriella's heart was racing and I could sense her pulse in my hand!

Geoff got some stones and immediately rushed toward us, throwing the big stones at the sheep. He hit a few with his stones, and the sheep got scared and ran back to the hillock in panic. Geoff came down and gave hand to Gabriella to bring her down and I climbed swiftly down. "That was a close call mate," chipped Geoff. Indeed, it was, considering the speed at which the Bharals came for us. We walked fast towards the other side of the stream and proceeded to a small valley formed by short hillocks. I commended Gabriella for her swift run and she shot back, "I am a Pilates trainer and a Yoga practitioner, man!" We continued our exploration and reached the tent back by early dusk. The tea was ready and the cook was all smiles for us with the snacks.

The painters of the Universe began making way for dusk. The canvas of the sky began getting painted red from the west. Few ravens flew in and sat beside our kitchen tent in anticipation of some food. The cook came with snacks and tea, we assembled in front of the ladies' tent laying few sleeping mats, sans Geoff who went to his tent as he had his menu prepared by his cook. Bella was curious as to why the sheep attacked us, and Gabriella quipped, "Because they loved us!" Bella poked her and asked me the same question, and I told because the sheep could not reach Bella and Geoff. She got completely irritated and kicked me! Pleasantries continued and we spoke of our travel stories and personal lives for a good one hour, by the time it really turned cold.

The cook came and announced that the dinner would be served after an hour and a half. I got my jacket and sleeping bag and asked Tenduk to come after one hour for dinner, but Tenduk told me he had some packed food so he would have it there itself. I returned to Bella's tent and asked if we could play cards or listen to music. Gabriella responded that music would be great, and she had her Bluetooth speaker and memory card, iPod, backup power bank etc. She put it in a jiffy and we started to settle around inside their tent. The music played over the next one hour was jazz and blues. I got the cards out after 10 minutes and we started playing a few commonly known games. The games were accompanied by witty conversations and a lot of leg pulling. In about an hour the cook came to call for dinner, and we proceeded to the kitchen tent. Meanwhile I decided to get something from Geoff's tent as well. Geoff was having dinner in his kitchen tent and gave me a gravy to add on to my dinner. I took it to the other kitchen and we sat down for a lavish dinner. I offered to pay for it, on which Bella gave a whack on my head and asked me to start the dinner.

We had a good sumptuous dinner courtesy the talented cook of the ladies. I finished the dinner and bid the girls good night saying am going to do some star gazing or astronomy. Gabriella told she will join if she feels like after the dinner. I went to my tent and fetched my Nikon star gazer binoculars for some astronomical observation. I looked above and saw a myriad of infinite stars and constellations. Thank God it was a clear sky night in spite of the snow in the day time. I could see the full moon clearly on the eastern horizon shining its borrowed glory from Sun, on us mortals on this green emerald planet.

I felt as though this mountain was my space shuttle and that I had got out at that point to feel the expanse of the sky's infinity and mystery. I sighted the Pleiades star constellation popularly known as the Seven Sisters. There was a special star among the Pleiades called Karthika or Krttika star as per Hindu astronomy and astrology. This is a star related to Lord Karthikeya of the Hindu pantheon of Gods, he is a God of self-knowledge and enlightenment. He also is the War

General of the Devas or Gods. Coming to Pleiades, it is 444 light years away from our planet; and imagine the light from that star cluster falling on me. What ecstasy! You might be thinking I am mad, but yes unless you turn a bit crazy you can't be aware or observe such a sidereal phenomenon beyond the cliched dimensions of this earthly realm. I wondered at that moment if astronauts felt the same way when they discover or sight something unique. At that moment Gabriella walked in alone and nudged me enquiring what I found. I narrated my thoughts, and she started laughing nonstop for a couple of minutes. I laughed along as well, and then told, "jokes apart but don't you think the world has always found new ways and has been redefined only when people think like this and go exploring?!"

She laughed again, and asked, "So you are the new Galileo, eh?! Sir, please enlighten and educate me please!" I grinned and continued, "think about the infinity of this Universe, and then there are so many other infinite numbers of Universes; now let's take only this Universe, think how many infinite galaxies are there which the science has postulated and found out to an extent, in that we are in a small galaxy called the Milky way which itself is a million light years. Our solar system is located in the Milky Way, a barred spiral galaxy with two major arms, and two minor arms. Our Sun is in a small, partial arm of the Milky Way called the Orion Arm, or Orion Spur, between the Sagittarius and Perseus arms. Now we are in a speck called the Solar system; and that too we are in one of the tiniest specks called "Earth" within that 'so called' Solar system speck

- further in a continent, then a country and then a region, and we have the audacity to think that we know all and have figured it all out??!! That's all my honor."

Gabriella held her palms on her face in astonishment with wide eyes and an open mouth. She lifted the hands half bent and bowed to me three times and said, "My dear Professor of Astronomy and Space science, I bow before your highness. Please pardon my statements, will ya?!" And I burst into laughter, realizing I just roasted her processing brain! She came close and asked me, "Where did you learn all these stuff man?" I quipped that I would complete it and then let her know. She was ok with that and asked me to continue.

I continued, "this is about the absolute zero, the weird yet wonderful concept of time, how are we humans even using the concept of time. Are we doing it right or rather are we perceiving it right. We have used time to establish years, and if that is a true concept, what if someone goes beyond the earth's sun-based time zone? Would they not be affected by age?" She pondered and signaled me that her brain was going in rounds. We smiled and I said, "Wait let me explain it to you with your thought process – think if you start travelling from India in flight to US or Canada on a particular day, and say you arrive after two days, but you would notice that the date is the same and time more or less the same. So, what happened to the calendar time, where did the time go in transit; you arrived after all this travel on the same day. So, how do you explain the time construct my lady?!" She nodded and asked me for a break, drinking a couple of mouthfuls from her water bottle and asked me to pause. Then she told, "Rath, I have always wanted to date a handsome Indian; and now you are good looking and with heck a lot of brains, and I don't know if we would meet after this trip. So, I want to give it a start by kissing you, you maverick!"

She gave me a good passionate smooch and I was caught unawares; I started pleasantly reeling and enjoying the delightful moment and reciprocated it in equal and more intensity. That went for more than a few delightful minutes and then we just got aware, she continued hugging me and said that she was very happy that she could have a great outing to the Himalayas with her good friend, and find new friends and experiences. I too was delighted that at least someone listened to the non cliche topics and loved me for who I am. I adjusted my gloves and told her that I will show you something amazing and used my binocs to zoom in on the moon and showed it to her. She loved it but said that she had seen these kinds of views, "show me something special dear". I took the binocs back and showed the Orion star cluster, explaining that it's got a belt called 'Orion Belt' and there is a Nebula in between. Also, there are stars called Betelgeuse, Meissa, Bellatrix, Saiph and Rigel which form the hunter kind of constellation pattern. And what makes the belt are Alnitak, Alnilam and Mintaka."

She interrupted, "Rath keep it simple please, I am a physio doc not a Nasa person!" I caught her and gave her a good shake come hug followed by a kiss on her forehead and said, “Now it will go in babe!” She relished it and blushed, and told that, “yes, it’s going in my head! Hey is anyone observing?” And she turned back to our tents. We looked back and saw that Geoff was conversing with Bella on the chairs put outside. I continued, “so, Alnitak is around 800 light years away from earth and is 100,000 times more luminous than our Sun. Alnilam is approximately 2,000 light years away from Earth, and with ultraviolet light is 375,000 times more luminous than the Sun. Mintaka is 915 light years away and is 90,000 times more luminous than the Sun. I stop at that Gab, now you understand the depth and wonder of the subject matter?!”

She clapped and told me that she would have given me a medal and certificate if we were down in the plains. I grinned and asked that right there, and she gave me a sweet peck on the cheek! She continued, “ok so that means what we learn in school and college is just scratching the surface of the subject matter and we probably live our commercial/materialistic lives ticking the checklist and doing maintenance of our existence till we die and it does not make any difference. This really is deep stuff Rath, thanks for enlightening and throwing some light on celestial wonders; I will go back and research more.”

I felt like the stars were floating around me, celebrating with me the moment of bliss in terms of the observation and also meeting this firangi girl who was a good listener, which I never even dreamt of. Those moments were truly magnificent and magical!

I, for one, would cherish that for this life, considering I was a bachelor at that time, more reasons for it to be registered into the deep recesses of the mind. She signaled we could walk to the pond and sit for some time, before retiring to the tents for the night. I obliged and we walked to the pond, meanwhile there was a mildly cold breeze adding joy to the ambiance. As we were walking, I said, "You wanted to know how I learnt all these, right? See, I have always been a wanderer and wonder personified guy thinking about the deeper - seldom answered realms and areas of life. For instance, I study Indian philosophy and metaphysics and started wondering about time and other dimensions which we were made to forget from college or university times, unless you pick a similar topic for graduation like astrophysics or space stuff. So, I started learning about astronomy from the books, internet, online videos and started experimenting with it in the night sky in the city as well as places I travelled to; slowly over the last 8 years I have learnt something to make me happy and also differentiate me from the regular crowd!

Gabriella patted me and asked, "What are your other hobbies, baby?" I was delighted, for I was getting applause and fandom from a smart, adventurous and beautiful foreigner girl that too with some brains; whereas I used to hardly get any listeners down in the city I lived for conversations, as people were hardly interested in sidereal stuff like this.

"Photography, Hiking, Rookie Bouldering, Naturalism, Reading, Writing, Music, Muscle building,

Yoga, Cycling, Adventure sports, Philosophy, History, Archaeology, Healing, Exploration, Birding, self-improvement etc." I jested with a wink! Gabriella got irritated in a fun way and said, "have you left anything man? Enough of you, now let me talk about myself, am a girl or lady whatever; I need to brag as well, you jackass." We reached the pond by then and sat there. She said, "I am a practicing physio as you know with interests in Pilates in which I am a certified trainer, History and Museums, Adventure sports, Ballet dancing, ice skating, watching TV, shopping like any girl, reselling antiques, pubbing, gun shooting etc. So, I am equally good man, yeah! And yes we got some common interests as well, you see."

I bowed to her and gave a nudge on her head. She continued by narrating a few stories from her hobby lives, and I sat with rapt attention. When a girl is on roll in bragging, the best thing is to be all ears and I just followed that protocol. She was from Louisiana, New Orleans and had shifted there a year back from Dallas due to better employment offers. She went on, "New Orleans is world-renowned for its distinctive music, Creole cuisine, unique dialects, and its annual celebrations and festivals, most notably Mardi Gras. The historic heart of the city is the French Quarter, known for its French and Spanish Creole architecture and vibrant nightlife along Bourbon Street. So, you see where my love of music got boosted. You got to come there man; I would love be your host if you come down this year, and we could have a lot of fun you know!"

I smiled and said, "Babe, it takes a lot of money for me - to and fro!" She offered me full sponsorship when I was there, but then was helpless with the flight charges. I nodded and said, "Let me see, Gab". She was all smiles and blurted out that she is single now and free apart from the work engagement. That was a sign of invitation, I thought to myself; but where on earth am I going to find the money to sponsor myself?! Back at that time I was not earning big, just enough to support my EMIs and travels. So international travel was a big question mark. Nevertheless, I sat all ears, meanwhile I untied my shoes and put my legs in the water; to which she warned me that it was very cold and I could get frostbitten feet. I ignored and continued my tom foolery.

Suddenly I got a sensation as if something soft and considerable touched under my feet with some force, I jerked and got shocked! "What happened?", squeaked Gab. "There was something under my feet in the water, there was a thrust of something soft yet sturdy; I could feel it, I don't know" I told. Pulling my leg and rubbing it with the towel I had in my sling bag, I felt silent and thinking. "What was it, what do you reckon it could be?", she enquired. I really had no clue and I remained silent. We just moved a few feet away and sat, she kept patting on my back. After a few moments, she spoke of her future travel plans along with the next visit to India as a way to change the topic. As that time in April was not a good time to visit south of India, she wanted to complete most of the major north India and return. She insisted, "we must meet when I will be down south of India next year, keep yourselves free, you are going to be my host; I will intimate you in advance, Rath." I nodded with a big grin and welcomed her.

But my mind was still stuck with the thing which touched my sole of the feet, and kind of gave a thrust after holding for a second probably. I blurted, "that thing felt as soft and rubbery as a big snake head probably, I am assuming this because I am also a hobby herpetologist Gab". "Are you crazy Rath? How can there be such a thing in a small pond? You are hallucinating! And don't tell me you catch snakes, man", she exclaimed. "I do catch them girl, not for fun but as part of rescue and release, I have a great liking to the study of snakes!" She was in disbelief, as she quipped, "I can't stand that creature - it feels and looks slimy and am totally averse to that Rath; now, don't narrate any story of snakes, let's leave that topic please." But I told myself – "I definitely was not hallucinating", and later that evening after we went to the tents, I woke up in the middle of the night and came again to check that. The experience I had then was a massive and mystical one, which I am keeping for the future as a separate mystical thriller story!

Coming back, we again looked at the stars and realized a lot of time had passed, giving each other a big hug and a kiss we went back to the tents for sleep. She went to her tent and I went to mine, and lay down in my sleeping bag, pondering of what it could have been. I could recall that just before that, I had seen a bubble and some movement just beside my leg which I had ignored. I could not get much out of the thinking, so I kept thinking about Gab and gradually went to a deep sleep soon after. The middle of the night adventure is for another book as already this story is very long.

I got up at 6 am and went out and started stretching myself, and saw that Geoff and Bella were doing Yoga on their sleeping mats outside the tent. Gab was not to be seen, so I went looking for Tenduk but could not spot him either. I went up to Geoff and greeted him good morning. Geoff asked me to take a seat in his tent, and ordered the cook to get me a black tea. I thanked him and winked at Bella, she blushed and continued her Yoga. They were doing Suryanamaskars as that would heat up their cold bodies in the morning. I went to the kitchen and got some hot water to wash my face and mouth. Freshening myself I came back to find my tea just ready. Sipping tea at the top of a glacier in the early hours, watching firangis doing Yoga is just a pleasure and also a whack on us Indians, as to how much the firangis love and understand Yoga more than us Indians. I am asking, tell me if any Indians in such a situation while camping would do Yoga in the morning? No is the answer, so I got a great motivational whack that morning and decided that I will also start the Yoga I knew and left a few years back.

Just as I was lost in my thoughts, Gab came out of her tent and greeted me good morning with a nice sweet bubbly hug sky rocketing my oxytocin levels! She also sat down for a tea, and as we were sipping our tea the Sun came out of the clouds and that just brightened all of us. We chatted for a while about last night and the sleep; and by the time Geoff and Bella finished their yoga practice, we immediately started our short practice facing the Sun and Shivling Mountain inspired by Geoff and Bella and boy what an amazing feeling it was to open the body, breath, mind, energy and soul to the Himalayas with a good company!

We finished our super Yoga come Pilates session and joined the two of them along with Tenduk for breakfast. Gab gave me some crash lessons on Pilates. Let me put one thing in perspective here, these foreigners were so large hearted and open that they never differentiated between me and my porter who did not have a kitchen; rather they embraced us as their own close friends and offered fantastic hospitality which I have not seen with many Indians. We tend to have narrow minds and be exclusive, we only talk about inclusivity whereas firangis practice it from their heart, a big bow to them. We soon finished our breakfast and got ready for a small hike towards Nandanvan. Just then from the adjacent small peak we saw a herd of blue sheep or bharals coming down, the girls got scared and immediately went back to their tents. Geoff and I stood looking, Tenduk was busy searching for something. The bharals started coming down towards us and the girls started calling us in panic. Just then as the bharals were nearing in more speed Tenduk started banging a stick on a big 2-liter bottle producing loud beats. The bharals stopped and kept looking for a moment, and Tenduk started walking towards them. Interestingly the bharals turned left and ran away as if fearing something. We all were relieved considering their size and strength. The girls came out and shook hands with Tenduk and Geoff gave him a much-deserved pat. I praised him stating, “he is a mountain expert, it comes naturally to him!” Tenduk grinned like a child and kept the bottle in his bag and told us to start immediately.

We started our hike and proceeded towards the beautiful valleys ahead leading up to Nandanvan. Nandanvan was not our destination as we did not have the entire day for that trek. So, we went through the glaciers and crevasses enroute to just get a wider picture and experience of the deep glacier hike experience. And I can say without an iota of doubt that it was mesmerizing and incredible. The softness of the snow, the toughness of the glacier and in between ice all was a delightful first-time experience for me, sans for the others as they had seen it before. So, I was like a child enjoying all of these. The others were walking in front of me conversing about the Himalayas. Tenduk was leading the way and he took us till a small mountain from where he showed us the iconic Nandanvan and Vasuki Parvat. We all were really jubilant and blessed to experience this pristine wonder of deeper Himalayas, and sat down. We were well inside the Gangotri national park. Gab posed a question, “do we have snow leopards or any animals here?” “I don’t think so, apart from the blue sheep we saw”, quipped Geoff. I told her she was a beautiful animal to look at, on which she gave me a kick! I laughed and asked Tenduk his opinion, he said that there are some fishes in the streams and waters but nothing apart from that. Surprised, I asked, “can they survive in this cold”? Tenduk nodded his head and said that there are also some migratory birds which are somewhat big in size. That was an interesting revelation, pondering that all sat silent for some time. Geoff got busy clicking pics around and the ladies joined in; after some time, Tenduk told us that we should head back, pack our tents and leave for the base ashram before it becomes dark.

We unpacked our snacks, slowly relished it and hit the route via the glacier back to our tents. Conversing on future Himalayan hiking and mountaineering plans, we reached in under two hours at Tapovan and went for some rest in the tents. Subsequently Tenduk and other staff packed the tents and were ready to go. We sat for a few minutes soaking it all in before going back, Geoff was again busy with photographs. So, I took the time to chit chat with the girls. It was around 3 pm and we soon started our descent from Tapovan. The hike down from Tapovan to Gomukh was very steep giving some real strain in the knee for all. In around an hour we were in Gomukh, refreshed ourselves, clicked a few solo and group pics, me and Bella, me and Gab and with Geoff. The ladies took another 15 min for their poses and snaps before we got going. In 3 hours, we were at the base ashram and having our tea. Majority of the guests we saw 2 days back were there, discussing their respective adventures and perspective on what they saw and experienced. We became a group and sat in Geoff's dormitory for a good one hour sharing our contacts and details.

Next day we boarded to Rishikesh, where Geoff parted ways, Tenduk was paid and set free in Uttarkashi and I joined Gab and Bella for 3 days of Rishikesh exploration, where we had a lot of fun exploring cafes, shops and ghats of Rishikesh. We explored a lot of Yoga centers and temples as well. Bella was a good artist, so she sketched a lot of places like ghats and the people in streets especially Sadhus. She also sketched me and Gab sitting in the cafes, and gave it as a souvenir to me. I gifted few Indian cloth materials to both, as they had now become lifelong friends. After 3 days I bid adieu to the lovely hearted ladies and returned to Bangalore back to the corporate world. Myself, Gab and Bella are still friends and I met them when they came to India again the following year.

I returned with a truck load of life long memories and good times to last me a year of reminiscence, until the next major trip to Himalayas.

# Crocs of Bheemeshwari!

I am going to take you now to 2008 before the recession began. One of my office friends Pankaj and I were discussing going for a ride on the weekend. My friend being from North India and new in Bangalore was not aware of places nearby, so I suggested a place I had gone before called Bheemeswari located 100 km from Bangalore in the Cauvery Fishing Camp area. It is located in Malavalli taluk, Mandya District. A wonderful mix of delightful nature and wild adventure, this camp is close enough for easy access and far enough to cut yourself off from the everyday humdrum.

When you travel on the Kanakapura road for exactly 80km crossing Kanapapura town, you would come about a deviation to the left with a tourism sign board of Cauvery fishing camp, which will take you to a place called Bheemeshwari named after a temple Goddess in the forests of Muttathi. Bheemeshwari is a forest settlement of a few villages who live doing farming and fishing. These people also double up as forest guides and watchmen when needed. We were riding down to this place on bikes passing beautiful lush green pastures before Bheemeshwari arrived; progressing into villages and forest department check posts before reaching the destination. It is a quaint little settlement with many coracles laid aside, used by locals for fishing. I hardly knew the length and breadth of the Cauvery River flowing here and that there were crocodiles in plenty.

We arrived by the village area where the coracles were lined up and vehicles were parked and strolled around exploring the place. There were few small shops and local houses. We walked towards the water body at the end of the wide mud road adorned with big old trees. The river was a beautiful expanse of a big water body flowing in subtle tranquility. We walked along the river towards the west soaking in the beautiful breeze, observing the bird life that was flying around. There were few kingfishers and mynahs sitting around anticipating prey, just then a grey hornbill flew by and sat on a branch nearby. Calling out loudly it drew our attention exclusively, we were seeing a hornbill for the first time so did not know the name until we came back and searched it out. We continued the walk, passing through many ancient and huge trees standing magnificently in water, as along the bank in that area the river flow was less and more or less it was stagnant water. There were many monkeys hopping from tree to tree, squeaking in unison, I spotted couple of species at least.

We walked a little further and saw that there was no way ahead but to go through deep water, so we turned back and walked past a nalla to reach the place we began. After buying water and snacks we picked up our bikes and went further ahead not knowing where it was leading. Shortly we came to the gate of Cauvery Fishing Camp which was closed. It was written that it was allowed for only guests who had booked in advance. So, we did not waste much time and went a bit ahead, riding through the half forest which was prevalent along the sparse settlements and odd temples for the forest deity. Just as we passed an open small stony temple for a Goddess, we saw a dog-like thing; I called out for Pankaj to stop. We stopped and looked back; the thing was a fox! It was looking out for probably another fox or its pack. We both had seen one for the first time in life, so our excitement was quite obvious. Pankaj took out his point and shoot camera and clicked a few images. The tail was a trademark bushy one and the body was small and slender.

Once upon a time this animal was a household story as it was there in every village and bushy forest adjoining human settlements. Slowly owing to the chicken and goat snatching by the fox, which affected the basic animal farming of people it was hunted down or driven away. Over a period of time their habitats were lost to towns and cities and their population dwindled to now being an endangered species.

We rode a bit towards it on the opposite side of the road, to get a closer picture; but it sensed us and ran away in a hurry. Just then a villager who was observing us came forward and told us in Kannada that they are usually shy and less in number, and very afraid of people. So, we asked him, "what else do you see commonly over here?" He said the jungle fowl; peafowl are the ones commonly found and they are good food for these foxes. He also said that there was the occasional panther or leopard which frequented the place, and preyed on spotted deer or jungle-sheep. We got a bit scared, seeing us taken aback he immediately said, "nothing to worry in the day time, only in the night don't go out alone." This cooled us a bit. He directed us to visit an area a bit further ahead, where from the shore we could see crocodiles. This got us interested, and we bid adieu to the villager and went ahead for a croc sighting adventure.

As we approached the area, he had described we could clearly see a clearing where we could park our bikes and go for the adventure. We went ahead and parked our bikes there and went to the shore to sight the crocs. We could see only water and a couple of islands in them. Turning to Pankaj I told, "nothing's there here bro". Let's walk a bit further along the shore; we did exactly the same and we came across two guys, one an extremely dark-skinned guy with unkempt messed up hair and the other one an average dusky guy. Both were observably drunk and stinking to an extent. They greeted us and asked us why we were there. We told them to watch the crocs from the shore. They laughed at this and told us that to observe the crocs up close - we need to go into the water, to the island located further ahead; but for that we need to take their help as there were many whirlpools in the river which only they knew. They could help us move through safe route to the island and spot some crocs. So, we asked them how much would they charge and spot came the reply 100 each. That was kind of ok for the adventure in store, so I discussed with Pankaj and we consented to giving it. But we asked them about their identity and they revealed a shocking profession – that they were dead body lifters deployed by the forest department as there were at least couple of deaths every month of tourists who got down into the Cauvery River and got lost in the whirlpools. So, they were deployed there from 9 am to 6 pm to warn tourists and also help if somebody was caught drowning. That was quite some information and also a very dangerous profession indeed.

They asked us to fold the pants and get ready to get down. We started in earnest, getting down into the thigh deep water catching on few branches of a tree protruding into the river. The flow was considerable but not dangerous. I was the one who understood and knew Kannada among us, so Pankaj asked me to lead following the instructions of the guys. I walked in front and in front of me was one of the dead body lifters and the other guy speedily swam across to the island. We progressed cautiously wading through tree debris and hip deep waters towards the island and reached the island in around 20 minutes. I for one was very delighted to step into a crocodile island as told by the guys, it was something of a movie kind of experience in real life. I had only seen crocs in zoos in an enclosure from a safe distance. Now, we were in their habitat and one could be around the corner.

*Cauvery river flowing through Bheemeshwari*

The aerial view of Cauvery fishing camp near Bheemeshwari is something like amazon river with deep thick forests on both sides, with many small islands interspersed in the river. Now, the entire island we were on was covered with a special kind of beautiful bouquet grass adding beauty to the look of the island in the middle of the river. The flowing water was adding to the beauty of the entire ambiance. Just then the other guide guy shouted out calling for us, we rushed immediately. He showed us a croc around 50 m from where we were, it was literally a shocker considering it could anytime swim to its home. The other guy was missing; I looked around and asked the guy with us; he said that the other guy had gone for picking crocodile eggs while this guy was watching out for the croc. This shook both me and Pankaj and we expressed disbelief and asked why would they do that. He said that they would take it ashore to make an omelette out of it, and was very tasty as per him; Pankaj let out a yuck expression and he immediately ran towards where we came from. I went to check the guy stealing the eggs after having a good view of the croc and ensuring that it was facing the other side.

I saw that the dark guy collected 3 eggs and was checking it by shaking, ensuring it was a recent egg eligible for being an omelette! I was furious at the same time scared if the croc rushes by. He loaded his polythene bag with 3-4 eggs and signaled the other guy with him; Pankaj was waiting at the end where we set foot on the island, just ready to escape in case the croc turns up and attacks. The dark guy went up to his friend and both stood observing the croc. Myself and Pankaj explored the area of the island we were standing in and found few big fishes washed ashore and few others probably the croc had caught as food. We took few pics with the big fishes posing as if swallowing it, something like the 'dil chahta hai' movie kind of pic. I then thought of checking the guides as we didn't see them for quite a while. I saw both of them throwing stones at the croc afar, which was suicidal to say the least. I got mighty angry and called out to them, "eno nann makkalra namna sayisokke plan madidheera? (what you bloody guys have planned to kill us, is it?)" I reprimanded and shouted at them badly, for one - abusing the animal, second creating danger when all was safe. They came back, but I saw the croc swimming towards the island and I shouted; and all of us ran back. Something in me told to wait and check the croc, so I turned back and observed from behind a rock – the croc was steadily heading towards us! It was a big one, my mouth opened in awe and fear. It could easily charge at us once on the island, as it was about to reach the island, I ran with all my might signaling the others to start back.

*Indian Crocodile in the river*

If the croc found out about the eggs and we were still on the island, we would be minced meat for sure. So, first Pankaj got into water followed by the guides and then me. We waded quickly through the water and took a good 20 min to reach the shore. I and Pankaj let out a big sigh of relief and turned back to see if the croc was visible; the croc was not visible but we walked a ten meter up and saw the tail of the croc sticking out. Coming back Pankaj gave his piece of mind in Hindi to the guide guys, I don't know what they understood but they bent their heads and told in Kannada that they were drunk and liquor made them do the mischief of throwing stone. I gave both of them combinedly 100 and told as they were there for eggs than guiding us and because of the risk they put us in, I can give only that much and left. They kept calling us to give another 100, but we ignored and walked away.

Reaching our bikes we straightened our pants and picked the helmets and rode away to Bangalore highway remembering the adventure and the paranoia of seeing the big crocodile up close at its home. Pankaj and I discussed our own point of views during ride breaks and reached home before midnight and called it a memorable thrilling day, looking forward to another such adventure in the near future.

# DEEP IN THE HOGENAKKAL FORESTS!

Welcome to the final story of the book where I take you to the pre corona year of 2019, with a camping story in the wild Hogenakkal bordering Karnataka and Tamilnadu states. This is a story where we camped inside the jungles adjoining the Cauvery River which had sand dunes island on one side and deep forests on the other. We encountered elephants and a special guest which I reveal as the encounter story unfolds.

I had been to Hogenekal with my wife and kid in Jan 2019 for an outing, where we took the coracle and went exploring inside the river experiencing the beautiful sand dunes and their beauty. This fascinated me so much that, I asked the coracle driver if he can take me inside these kind of places for a camping. He was in the affirmative, but said that not all islands are accessible due to the restrictions imposed by forest department. But he could take me to a place which is feasible if I can give the exact dates for him to get the permission from the forest department. So, I went back and discussed with my office colleagues about the prospect and got their consent and interest. I gave him a date and he got the needed permission from the forest department to camp in a place where not much wildlife encounter was there.

We reached Hogenakkal waterfall parking area by evening and the coracle guy was waiting with his friends for us. The sun hung low over the horizon, casting its final amber glow over the dense canopy of Hogenakkal. The coracle guy told us we needed 3 coracles as there are 9 of us and we need to head fast before it gets dark. We started immediately, but we had to take some snacks and raw items to cook. So, we asked him to take us to some shop in the town. He got us to the town and we got the necessary provisions but needed some masala also for cooking; so, I told him some masala is needed. He immediately asked me to follow him on the car, and he took us to a shop. Looking at the shop I was surprised and puzzled as it was a chicken shop. I enquired as to why he brought us there, as we had no intention of taking non-veg. He replied that, "you only told you want masala, so I brought you to the masala shop; take as much chicken as you want". It took me a while to figure out to my amusement that chicken is what they refer to as masala in that part of the world! I and my friends Uday and Rakesh had a good laugh before asking him for a normal grocery shop. Purchasing the things needed we boarded their autos laden with the coracles and headed towards the forest. There were 3 autos and enroute the coracle guy got the nod from the forest guys at a check post and took us inside.

We parked the autos at a particular place and started following the coracle riders. It was getting dark and we needed to reach the camp spot before the dusk fell. Now, the challenge was to run fast and cross many of the intermediate water bodies using the coracle and get to the main spot.

We ran fast, boarded the coracles when the water was deep and waded through the water streams when it was shallow; and after crossing many a water streams reached the camping spot at the nick of time when it was about to be dark. The place was a river beach with very smooth sand and I just loved the ambiance. The river in front of us flowed deeper and majestically with the forest on the other shore. This shore was our beach and the temperature was normal unlike the cold we expected. The coracle guy said that he will get some firewood for the camp fire before it goes complete dark. On asking, he said that he will only pick or cut the wood from fallen trees. He went about his business and I went about mine getting the guys to help me set up the three tents equidistant from the campfire spot. My friend Ravi and I started to set up the tent with practiced ease as we were the experts, the nylon fabric snapping crisply as we pegged it down. The air was rich with the scent of trees and wild jasmine, with the occasional call of a Malabar whistling thrush echoing from somewhere deep in the forest. It was serene… almost too serene. As soon as we were done, the coracle guy brought the big logs of wood and set up the camp fire. The bonfire was an absolute stunner, its flames licking the night sky with a crackling intensity. Sparks danced upwards, swallowed by the canopy above. We skewered fresh vegetables onto sticks, roasting them over the flames. The sizzling sound of dry veggies hitting the fire was hypnotic, blending with the bubbling melody of the river. We danced for some time around the fire soaking in the forest atmosphere and the river beside. Rakesh and Uday were the main cooks for the dinner. They were also cooking some rice, curry and then masala noodles.

While the food cooked, I brewed a pot of strong coffee, its aroma mixing with the scent of burning wood as the other few guys' continued dancing to their bluetooth speaker music. After a while we sat down for the food which we ate slowly, savoring each bite under a canopy of stars, the moon peeking through the leaves like a watchful guardian. The sky was a spectacle with a lot of stars showing out, like the ones in the big dipper and small dipper constellations. The night was alit with the light of the stars and the campfire.

Two sides of our camp were full of trees, one side that is the front side was the flowing river and on the other side a little afar was another team which had put up a tent and were cooking their dinner. We had picked the perfect spot for our camp right by the riverbank, surrounded by towering trees draped in nature's vibes; and vines that whispered secrets to each other in the evening breeze. For me, it was not just another camping which I had done in the wild, but different - as here rather than a mountain it was a river and river beach. For the other guys with me, barring three of them who had camped with me near Siddharabetta-Tumkur; it was a new experience.

Just before we were to finish the dinner, I told something to bring in some eeriness, thrill and interest into the group. "That river," I began, pointing a stick I had in my hand towards the shimmering water, "locals say it's cursed." My eyes gleamed with mischief, but my voice carried a note of seriousness. Ravi raised an eyebrow, and played along as I winked at him. "Cursed? How so?" "They say," I leaned in closer, my voice dropping to a whisper, "that at night, if you listen closely, you can hear whispers coming from the water... whispers of those who vanished in the forest." Sudarshan chuckled, brushing off my story as campfire theatrics. But even as he laughed, others felt a chill ripple through the air, one that had nothing to do with the night's coolness.

After the dinner was done myself, Rakesh and Uday went to the river to clean up the remains of our dinner when Uday suddenly paused, his eyes fixed on the tree line. "Did you see that?" he whispered. I turned, squinting into the darkness. At first, there was nothing - just the shadows swaying with the wind. But then, just for a flicker of a second, I saw them - two glowing eyes reflecting the firelight. They blinked once and disappeared.

"What was that?" Rakesh asked, his voice hushed.

"Leopard, maybe," I replied. "They're known to watch campsites from a distance." Although I knew it could be far from truth, wanted to put some excitement into the camping experience.

The thought of a silent predator watching us from the shadows sent a shiver down both of their spine. We all instinctively edged closer to the fire, its flames now seeming like the only shield against the creeping darkness. Couple of guys were drunk and retired into the tent, Ravi and Abhishek were out near the fire. Uday narrated his experience to them, and they were all ears and pretty wary of what they heard. So, I went up and gave a pat on both of their backs to lighten up the situation. "Let's catch whatever it is and roast it guys, what say?!" Which was returned with few chuckles and pleasantries.

We settled by the fire, the comfort of its warmth pushing back the unease. Hours passed as we chatted, the flames dying down to glowing embers. The river continued its endless journey, gurgling and whispering… and then it was about to be 12 am and we had planned to celebrate Sudarshan's birthday by giving him some dips in the river at midnight following it up with some birthday bumps. He was not aware of this plan which Ravi had suggested; so, we called Sudarshan and brought him to the river to show him something and then the guys lifted him without warning and dipped, him as many numbers as his age. The splashing of the river was like a DJ music and party fun. We brought him out lifted him and gave the birthday bumps, and put him down on the sand. Everyone poured in the wishes, with a birthday to remember and went together to take a dip in the river. Surprisingly in January when it should be really cold, the water was quite warm; so, the bath was a delight in the flowing shallow waters of January. This kind of birthday nobody would ever celebrate, even so rarely by a forest in a river at midnight. So, all thanks to the adventure of tenting and the place which give us such unforgettable memories which could last a lifetime.

The moon had shifted to the western horizon and was keenly observing us. We changed clothes and came back to the bonfire, barring three guys who were pretty drowsy and went to sleep, fire was rebuilt by the coracle guy. In the distance, the river's gurgling grew louder, more distinct - like murmurs threading through the night air. "Do you hear the river and some other noises?" Ravi asked, his voice excited.

I strained my ears. At first, it was just the usual sounds of the forest - the crickets, the rustling leaves but then, almost like a distant echo, I heard it - a whispering sound, soft and fragmented, drifting up from the water. It was impossible to make out what it was, but there were some unusual sounds along with the intermittent trumpeting of an elephant probably far off. The river shimmered under the moonlight, innocent and calm, as if all the sound were natural. But just as I turned away, I heard it again - an unusual sound, carried by the wind, something ambiguous. I could not figure out anything specific. I and Ravi discussed at some length as to the postulations of it, as we were the only really interested ones in nature, supernatural and adventure. After a while only the mellifluous flow of the river remained audible. We kept discussing travel stories across India, riding stories and then some supernatural stuff as Ravi had a lot of them in his kitty. The fire slowly rustled and broke as it was on the verge of silent smoky end. I went and called the coracle guy to rekindle the fire and put some fresh firewood, as it was a jungle we needed the fire as guardian all night long to keep the wild animals at bay.

The coracle guy soon refurbished the fire. By this time almost everyone except me and Ravi were in the tent and snoring the night away. Ravi also got some yawns and wanted to call it a good night, I obliged and we went to respective cozy tents to catch a good happy memorable nights' sleep. It took me a while for dozing off, meanwhile I was meditating on the next dawn's activities to the infrequent calls of the night jar. Looking forward to the long coracle ride across the Cauvery, from our camping spot to where we started initially, the coracle guy had told that it could be an hour and half before we could reach Hogenakkal parking. This was a pretty exciting thought to go to sleep with. I was happy that I could add another varied feather of camping on to my book of experiences.

*Our tents in Hogenekal forest near Cauvery River*

Next morning I and Uday were the first ones to get up before sunrise. I came out and was greeted with the chirping and flights of variety of birds all singing the morning glory and welcoming the Sun. Rakesh also came out of his green tent yawning big and hearty. Mist clung like magnet to the ground and river, and it was all a beautiful sight with the light break of dawn. We thought of going for a small trek on the path beside the tents into the woods. We washed our faces, drank some water, collected a bottle of water each from the river in case we had to answer nature calls, and started our small trek. As we wade through the semi dense fog and trees, the path narrowed and trees grew thicker. A 300m into the walk and lo we saw couple of elephants drinking water at the other end of the river further ahead, the tuskers however did not see us. We stopped to observe them in silence, squatting to the ground. A twig snapped behind us, the sound sharp and sudden. Then I heard it...

A hiss.

It was a distinct, elongated hiss, coming from the riverbank just a few meters away. Uday, Rakesh and I exchanged glances in sudden surprise. There it was - a considerably big cobra, its hood flared slightly, eyes fixed on us with an unnerving stillness. Its body was coiled partly in the dry leaves and twigs. We froze. The snake didn't move, its head swaying gently as if hypnotized by the flicker of the torch lighted by Rakesh. Finally, with a slow, deliberate motion, it slithered back into the dry leaves, starting to disappear beneath the surface without a sound. But I had a rare passion under my sleeves, being a herpetology enthusiast I did not want to leave the chance of an experience. Having handled and saved quite a number of snakes in the last couple of years in Choodasandra, Bangalore I wanted to give a try at this cobra; nothing but catching it, and leaving it a little far off. I passed a wink to the guys and picked a long stick lying around and emptied the cloth bag in which I was carrying the water and tissue papers. Rakesh and Uday were puzzled to their wits, as to what I was up to!!

I took out my torch a constant companion in camping, from the side pocket and switched it on in a jiffy pointing the beam directly to the snake's eyes. The snake turned into a statue, as it gets blinded. I started approaching slowly without making any noises. Snakes have no ears, but they compensate this by an acute sense of feeling. Through the scale upon their bellies that rest against the ground they are able to sense danger from anything that moves by detecting the vibration caused by that movement. So, I had to be extra careful approaching it. The boots I was wearing had soft rubber soles and I approached undetected barring for a light stamping on a twig when I was almost near the cobra. It hissed and attacked the ground; I took a step back and waited continuing the torch beam on its eyes. Snakes' eyes are lidless and fixed and cannot turn sideways or backwards, which made my job easy. The snake appeared to be fat around half a foot from its head, which I guessed to be some big frog swallowed in one piece.

*Indian Cobra or Naja Naja*

The sufficiently expanded skin in the region of its head showing the characteristic V-mark was clear and evident. Now, to catch this I had to use the stick in a fast motion and hold its head and pin it to the ground. I did it in a smooth movement changing the stick in my hands with dexterity; pinning its head to the ground with enough force not to harm it or leave it. One has to be quick to catch a venomous snake in particular considering the mortal risk. But there is really nothing to it apart from practice which I had in sufficient quantity. I quickly took the cloth bag which was somewhat thick and put it in front of the reptile, releasing that hand and quickly holding the stick with both hands, I moved the stick quickly to the one third area of the snake. Now, the snake had only one option, that is to get into the bag. It did just that in a moment and got into the bag in a hurry. I quickly lifted the stick and placed it at the mouth of the bag locking the entry of the bag. Now, as we herpers do - push the stick a bit further, so you can tie a knot at the mouth of the bag. I quickly tied the knot keeping the stick stamped at the neck of the bag. "The cobra is caught!" I shouted and looked towards the guys. They both were at least 20-25 feet away, gulping saliva with wide open eyes. "What bro, are you mad?" exclaimed Uday. I let out a big laugh releasing a slight tension I had. Rakesh just gave me a bow and told me to stay away. I held the bag pretty away from my body as the usual practice of herping goes and walked towards them. They ran away and stood at a good distance away from me.

I told, "let's walk little further and release this guy a little far lest any of our friends should walk in and shriek out. So, we continued our silent walk or you can call trek through the trees amidst a pleasant cool breeze carrying the songs of the birds. I told, "that's all is to catching a cobra. Some people have told me that it calls for nerve. Don't you believe that guys, in my opinion it is just the opposite; there should be 'no nerve', or as few as possible!" I said that I have tied the neck of the thick bag very firmly, after a pause we were back to our walk. Rakesh insisted we return soon as the others would be searching for us. I responded that I had informed the coracle guy that we would take a short while to return so don't worry about us; this silenced both of them.

After some considerable distance of our trek I stopped and told, "let's release this cobra in that bushes on the right which connects to a shrubby jungle growth.

Both of them acknowledged and I took the bag and placed its mouth towards the bushes. Slowly I patted the snake and it hissed, "bro careful", shouted Uday. I kept the stick at the neck of the bag and slowly untied the knot opening the mouth and, in a jiffy, lifted the stick and took couple of steps back. The snake did not move, so I poked it with the stick; in a sudden movement it slithered out and crawled into the bushes. Uday took few pics from his phone in the meantime and smiled, "bro I have captured Snake Ratheesh with Cobra, he he..!" I chuckled and we saw the snake disappear quickly.

On the left-hand side, on the other side of the river were few hillocks and pretty greenery. As we stood soaking it in, Rakesh wanted to return to the camp. We started walking back after the interesting adventure of the morning. By this time the mist had given way to some early warm sunshine. Let me put one thing in perspective here – life is all about adventure, and adventure involves calculated confident risk; if you do not create adventures in your life, trust me it's going to be a boring, dull life adhering to the routine and cliched way of living. So as much as possible think what is a good adventure I can do frequently, especially while travelling, so you create a great life filled with sparkling moments and great memories or stories. I believe in the famous quote, "Life is either a great adventure or a dull compromise"! Tom Cruise is one of the greatest inspirations in this respect, showing irrespective of age or circumstances we can live a daring, adventurous and special life if we heed to the thrills of Life.

We walked fast and reached the camp in 20 minutes. By this time Ravi and Abhishek were up and waiting for us. Ravi questioned, "where were your bro, you should have called me na?" Uday went quickly and showed his phone video to both. Both were taken aback and puzzled, Uday slowly elucidated the story and took both of them by surprise and unbelievable expressions. I left them and went ahead to wake other guys yet to wake from their hangover. These guys sleeping in tent - in the hangover of the overnight alcohol were hardly accustomed to adventure or camping and believed that liquor is the only way to celebrate life and they participated least in the adventures of the trip be it cooking or exploring nature, what a pitiable shallow lives; but I hope this experience created some impression on them to attune to the natural magic and intoxication of nature.

Soon, all were up and went ahead getting ready with their routine completion. Coracle guys also were ready with their coracles to get going. Uday and Rakesh the cooks quickly got cooking maggi for all. The pleasant smell of maggi is an aromatic splendor for any camping trip or adventure outing. I finished my quick stretches and Yoga asanas by this time and sat for the breakfast. All came around and we started our breakfast and enjoyed the quick conversations that followed. After which the tent dismantling and packing happened in a jiffy and we got going to the next adventure - the coracle ride in the middle of the forest, across Cauvery!

All of us crossing few streams got to the place where the coracle guys had planned to start the ride. We all got in and soon got going with all 3 coracles sliding across the river like a plastic ball. Sliding across the river we were enjoying the ride like kids pleasantly surprised by the beauty of the forests on both sides. Suddenly Padmanabhan screamed, "Ratheesh anna, see crocodiles!" I raised myself a bit and tried to see through the coracle in front and saw the tail of the croc swim into the water, towards the bank. We rode past quickly and all the guys were exchanging jokes around. Only me and Padmanabhan saw the croc and others were ignorantly aloof that they were riding among crocs. Cruising along we reached an area where there was a bank on the right side along with a lot of rocks from where one could do a good dive. So, we asked the coracle guys to stop there to take a plunge in the river.

The place was perfect for crocs to do sun bath as I thought, but there were none luckily. All of us got busy diving in the river and swimming around. There was a lot of silt in it, so we could not swim for much time. Coming out all applied body lotions and sunscreen and boarded the coracles. The coracle started passing through the beautiful Cauvery River with Karnataka forests on one side and lesser forest and road of Tamilnadu on the other side. The river stretched out before me like a shimmering ribbon of glass reflecting the sun. The breeze was strong yet therapeutic, one could just drift with it like in a fairy tale. A strong wave came about, the boat wobbled at first, sending tiny ripples fanning out across the surface, but soon it steadied, gliding gracefully with the current. Tall teak and mahogany trees stretched their limbs towards the sky on either side of the river, their leaves swaying lazily under the weight of the sun light.

Parrots squawked from the treetops, their bright green feathers blending seamlessly with the canopy until they took flight, cutting emerald streaks across the sky. Somewhere deeper in the woods, the haunting cry of a peacock floated through the air, rising and falling like a song caught on the wind. I was the one lost in this poetry of nature; the rest were making merry and chit chatting as the ride continued along the river with about 45 min left for us to reach the destination. I dipped my hand into the cool water, feeling the current tug gently at my fingers, as if the river itself were inviting me to follow its course. The coracle floated onward, spinning slowly with each paddle stroke, offering new glimpses of the landscape with every turn.

We sighted a family of spotted deer grazing quietly, their ears twitching at the slightest sound, eyes sharp and alert. One raised its head as I splashed a stone into the river, its gaze meeting ours for a fleeting moment before it vanished into the trees, its tail flicking off and vanishing. Further along the bank, I spotted the ruins of an old stone shrine, half-swallowed by creeping vines and tangled roots. It stood silent and forgotten, its moss-covered stones bearing the weight of years, watching the river flow by with eternal patience. It could be from the Vijayanagara period I presumed when these areas where under Hampi rule.

As the coracle meandered along the river's gentle bends, I felt a deep sense of peace settle over me. The river was a living thing - a silent storyteller, its waters carrying tales of monsoons and droughts, of fish that danced in its depths and birds that sang from its banks. It also carried the stories of so many generations and centuries of human history in its depths that if it were vocal, it could narrate great historical accounts that occurred over centuries. That was really a kind of sidereal thought for me, as the mystery that time has woven since time immemorial gives you a kick like no other if you delve into its intricacies and multi-dimensional perspectives.

Then suddenly a sound came - a distant roar, soft at first, growing louder with every paddle stroke. My eyes met the place where the river narrowed and the trees parted. I and other guys in the coracle leaned forward, to see what it was. And there it was - a waterfall, cascading down a series of rocky ledges, its waters sparkling like liquid silver. Ferns and wildflowers clung to the wet stone, their leaves glistening with droplets of water.

The coracle drifted closer, wobbling gently as the coracle man steered us towards a small, hidden inlet just to the side of the falls. We docked there, the coracle rocking slightly as we stepped onto solid ground. The roar of the waterfall filled my ears, also splashing the droplets on everyone's face. We explored the bank, careful with each step as the rocks were slippery with algae. Birds flitted overhead - parakeets, drongos, and even a pair of common oriental magpie robins that hopped from branch to branch, chirping curiously. It was around late morning 11 am and we were about to reach as the boatman told. The Sun was peaking now and all of them just wanted to reach as it was getting hotter. The river traversed many a curves and rocks with the expert riding of the boatmen. The guys in the coracle ahead were joking and making merry, the ones in the second ahead of me were silent barring one of them who was on a call, and the two guys in my boat were looking around in awe. In a while we were near the area, we had parked the vehicle in Hogenakkal town. All offboarded and walked towards our car, loaded the luggage and paid the boat wallahs with a big thanks, this all was over very soon as all were tired from the heat.

We started immediately as it was post noon, in our respective cars and drove through the beautiful route from Hogenakkal to Denkanikottai to Bangalore.

Thus ended one of the most beautiful camping stories with some memorable adventures in the jungle and Cauvery River.

-------------------------The End-------------------------

# ACKNOWLEDGEMENTS

My debts in getting this story off the ground and becoming an author are significant. First and foremost, I owe a deep thanks to all the great authors who kindled my deep reading interest over the years with observation, that matured into wanting to become an author.

I would like to thank my father for the good education provided, which put me on the pedestal leading to where I am today. I would like give a huge thanks to my wife Reshmi for providing the confidence, encouragement and being a reviewer of this humble work of the subject matter I love the most 'Nature & Wildlife'.

I am grateful to the first reviewers - my brother Ramesh, good friends Shanosh and Kodanda Ram, and Rajani S for providing some crucial feedback and inputs in bringing this dream to life. It reassured me that it was a story worth telling and sharing with the world, of my real-life camping experiences come stories in the jungles of India.

I am very grateful to Authors and Naturalists/Conservationists like Jim Corbett, Ruskin Bond, Kenneth Anderson, Ullas Karanth for they provided the motivation for penning something close to

Nature and Wild encounters. I am greatly indebted to all friends who have been part of the camping stories in this book and had contributed to some great memories in my life; specifically, my best friends Jacob Tom and Roshan Ali. Also, I would like to mention that without the great canvas of India and its mesmerizing wilderness and nature, this would not have ever been possible.

Very thankful to Bluerose Publishers and its staff for everything. Like to mention the Cover page, Editing, suggestions and their patience (Ankita and Sejal from Bluerose); as it took me some time to get the manuscript ready owing to few personal injuries. I am thankful for every bit of the production of this book being taken care of.

Reshmi and Mittu were my cheering squad. The support in the writing endeavour during weekends and late nights is very much appreciated. And, Reshmi thanks to reading multiple versions of the manuscript and providing key suggestions. A word of gratefulness to my sweet home, which provided me abundant ambiance in midst of Nature to write this close to the heart first book. And finally, thanks to the Universe and God Almighty!

# About the Author

Ratheesh Menon is an Explorer-Traveler, Spiritualist, Yoga teacher, Sound healer, Graphologist, Hiker, Mountaineer, Photographer, Entrepreneur and IT professional. He has been studying Yoga, Nature and Mysticism for the last 20 years and believes that Nature is the greatest spiritual teacher and healer.

Ratheesh is a die-hard believer that life's great mysteries can be unlocked only by an adventurous spirit and through Nature-Yoga combination (including finding purpose of life). His optimism and penchant for life spills from his own experiences and unique scientific yoga methods of exploring life.

He has lived in the greatest country on Earth - India, a Traveller at heart he considers it a blessing to live in this country and know so many stories indigenous to this land. He considers, his passion for Nature as one of his greatest blessings. In his free time, he can be found riding a cycle, Hiking in Western Ghats, doing breathwork, playing with family, meditating, reading books, working as a travel-tour operator or honing his skills as a polymath. His motto in life is "dive in, find yourself first – Like within, like without" all good things will follow!

Email Id: ratheeshm2112@gmail.com

Facebook: https://www.facebook.com/rathesshmenon

Instagram: https://www.instagram.com/rath_menon